FITNESS

Through *Active Lifestyle* and *Outdoor Pursuits*

FITNESS

Through *Active Lifestyle* and *Outdoor Pursuits*

José H. González, EdD

TABLE OF CONTENTS

INTRODUCTION

This professional development workbook starts with a review of the 3 main fitness components as they relate to outdoor pursuit activities (hiking, paddling, rock-climbing, etc.). This workbook has an online companion that can be accessed at www.ActiveLifestyleAndOutdoorFitness.com. The online companion has a list of tasks to complete, resources and guided questions for your own development as a fitness professional learning about how to integrate outdoor pursuit activities in your clients' fitness program design.

As a former Outward Bound instructor, I was responsible for creating experiences for my students that would compel them into value-forming ideas following the four pillars of Outward Bound: craftsmanship, self-reliance, service and physical fitness. As an instructor of 2-3 week-long sailing expeditions, trying to fit physical fitness in on land was hard. Sometimes we would go to the islands for a morning run and dip (in the cold water of Maine), however, most of the fitness occurred on the sailboat. The Outward Bound 30' sprit-rigged ketch had no engine; instead it had spots for eight rowers. On days with no wind, we would row for hours! As I reflect on those days, I was doing the equivalent of what I'd do at my local gym with a rowing machine to increase my cardiovascular endurance. Staying fit by doing outdoor activities or incorporating an active lifestyle, has always been my fitness approach. Nowadays, I take my dog and son for a walk or jog in the morning before going to work, or get on the water to surf or paddle.

Staying physically fit is a crucial aspect of staying healthy. Unfortunately, as you know exercise, for a lot of people, has become a dreaded activity that is meant to be forcefully done with only the end outcome of preventative measures taken or weight gain avoided as the end result in mind. While doing something is far better than doing nothing; if given an option, wouldn't every one of us opt for something that is inherently more enjoyable at the same time as being good for us? This is where physical fitness needs to become a part of one's lifestyle, something that a person eagerly looks forward to rather than fears. Every single moment of life is precious and should be enjoyed and cherished. There is absolutely no point in doing something that begins with a negative frame of mind. Either the mindset needs to be altered, or the activity needs to be changed. An active lifestyle that incorporates outdoor fitness training is able to achieve two strikes with one throw. There are few who have not enjoyed running on a sandy beach at sunset, or hiking or strolling beside a stream of water, or riding a bike over a mountain ridge. Not only do such fun-filled activities provide leisure & entertainment, they also lead to improved physical fitness, as well as an overall sense of well-being.

In recent years, there has been a proliferation of fitness facilities across the globe. It is not difficult to trace the reasons for this development. As people have become more and more busy in their work lives, they have compromised their health. This has manifested in the form of health problems such as cardiovascular problems, obesity and diabetes. Over the last few years, greater awareness of the link between physical inactivity and these lifestyle diseases has led to people contemplating making healthier choices such as participating in exercise routines. To make it conducive for people, gyms and fitness centers have opened up to provide them with avenues to perform physical workouts within the existing constraints of space and time. While this would be perfect under circumstances when a person enjoys his or her time spent in the gym; for many people though, this is not the case. All of the attention on the end goal of better health, in terms of objective parameters, has tampered the sheer joy of physical activity. This is where outdoor activities are much better, since they are oriented toward a different dimension—pleasure and enjoyment. The fitness and health benefits are secondary results from the joyful experience. Moreover, enjoyment ensures that there are greater chances of adhering to the activity as part of a lifestyle over a long period of time. There are numerous choices available as part of outdoor recreation that can be engaging and enjoyable for men and women of all ages. In addition, the benefits *are self-renewing/ self-fulfilling,* and endless, making one go out again and again, wanting more!

CHAPTER ONE

Benefits of Fitness Through Active Lifestyle and Outdoor Pursuits

The benefits that are derived from outdoor fitness activities include all of the benefits that accrue from participation in general fitness workouts. Around 150 to 180 minutes of moderate intensity, or 75 to 90 minutes of high intensity physical activity accumulated each week helps in maintaining a healthy body weight, lowers the risk of cardiovascular and coronary artery diseases, and prevents lifestyle disorders such as hypertension and diabetes to a large extent. In addition, there are numerous other benefits that are derived solely from outdoor activities. For ease of understanding, they have been classified under different headings.

PHYSICAL BENEFITS
Complete Physical Fitness Workout

There are a wide range of outdoor activities that a person can choose from. Apart from sports such as tennis, hockey, football and soccer, other physical activities include trail running, hiking, swimming, cycling, kayaking and stand up paddle boarding, to name just a few. The biggest advantage of these activities is that they provide a lot of variation and address the whole body. This ensures that all aspects of physical fitness such as cardiovascular endurance, muscular endurance, muscular strength, agility, power, flexibility, coordination, etc. are addressed in each workout. Each and every single one of these components is crucial for optimal physical fitness and therefore should be targeted.

Variation and Functionality

In addition to the aforementioned benefits, by including a variety of activities, the performance improves across multiple muscle groups, as well as across different functional movements. In case enough care is not taken while designing a workout routine, a gym workout plan may become one-dimensional that may not cover all bases. For this reason, of late, functional training has become an integral part of workout routines even in gyms; the aim is to mimic movements that are performed during normal functions and physical activities. A good mix of different outdoor activities inherently provides a complete whole body workout, thereby fulfilling any such needs.

Workout Efficiency

The workouts that are performed under normal outdoor conditions are more difficult than those performed in controlled internal environments. This means that the workout output and benefits of running outdoors can never be replicated by running on a treadmill. Research studies that have been conducted throw light on the fact that, for the same parameters (speed and gradient), the energy expended on a treadmill is lower than that expended while running outdoors. This may, perhaps, be due to the inherent running mechanism involved as well as due to increased drag or resistance experienced in outdoor conditions. A study in the late 90's conducted by scientists in the UK, stated that a 1% gradient accurately reflected the energy expenditure of running outdoors when speed and distance are same in both cases. Similar results have been seen in other activities such as cycling.

Vitamin D Synthesis

Vitamin D is an extremely crucial micro-nutrient that our body is able to synthesize. Not only does it prevent cancers and hormonal problems, but it also helps in better quality of life by helping to build a strong immune system and a body that is resistant to fatigue. However, Vitamin D can be produced only upon sufficient exposure to sunlight. Outdoor activities are really helpful in this regard, since it only seems logical that a greater amount of time spent outside shall lead to greater exposure to sunlight.

Access to Fresh Air

Despite the rising levels of pollution in the environment, exercising outdoors is still better than working out in an area that is poorly ventilated. Despite the claims of air conditioning and circulating units, they can never be a perfect substitute for fresh air that is available in a park or a forested trail. Oxygen is crucial to life and ready access to it during times of extra need is extremely important. In fact, working out in an atmosphere that lacks sufficient oxygen may not just be futile, it can be outright detrimental to health. By ensuring correct range of parameters such as outside temperature, humidity and altitude, maximum benefits can be leveraged by participating regularly in outdoor activities.

Physical Activity Benefits for Children

In light of the increasing issue of childhood obesity, it is imperative that children be introduced to physical fitness activities at a young age itself. To keep them engaged, it is essential that children enjoy participating in the activity. This is possible only through outdoor activities that are not monotonous in nature. Moreover, the activity should be such that they help in the growth and development of the bones without posing undue stresses. Working out in indoor setups with weights should not be considered since it may hamper with the development of the Epiphyseal plate thus jeopardizing bone growth. Outdoor activities that utilize body weight are more than sufficient for improving physical fitness in children.

Quality of Sleep

Numerous studies have shown that exposure to natural sunlight and fresh air helps in setting the biological clock in the body. This clock is what regulates our hunger and sleep patterns, by altering the hormonal secretion in the body. By participating in regular exercise in outdoor settings, our sleep patterns get normalized in a manner that greatly improves quality of sleep.

As can be easily observed, this has a pronounced positive influence on overall quality of life. Good sleep results in improved concentration powers and alertness, more energy and absence of sluggishness, all resulting in better performance across various facets of life.

PSYCHOLOGICAL BENEFITS
Motivation & Adherence

The biggest advantage of outdoor physical activities is that they are quite often leisure and recreation activities as well. This means that the person enjoys the experience and is not forced into participating in the activity. As a result, the person is self-motivated and therefore, the probability of adhering over a long period of time goes up considerably. Physical activity then becomes a part of the person's active lifestyle that has been adopted for life; it is not a short-term goal oriented activity that will be cast aside once the objective has been achieved.

Improved Mental & Emotional Health

Mental health and a positive attitude are equally important components of wellness. Indulging in physical activities performed outdoors has been observed to reduce stress, eliminate undue anxiety and prevent depression. It has in fact been seen to rejuvenate and have a calming influence on the mind. Feel good hormones such as *dopamine, serotonin and adrenaline* are frequently found to be at elevated levels; this leads to improved mood and a feeling of overall well-being. While impossible to measure objectively, these parameters definitely help in prolonging a good and healthy life.

Intellectual Benefits

Improved mental health, as discussed above, gets manifested in the form of increased confidence and better self-esteem. Learning a new skill to perform an outdoor activity offers intellectual stimulation and a sense of achievement. Improved creativity is what results; this, coupled with enhanced concentration power, leads to the intellectual productivity of the person going up. This further fuels the cycle that began with outdoor physical activity, leading to even better performance in work life.

Social Benefits

Outdoor activities provide a multitude of options that can be indulged in along with a friend or as part of a family or a group. These options are likely to keep a person motivated since they also provide an opportunity to socialize, one of the important needs of human beings. Very often outdoor activities performed with a partner, or as part of a group whose members are passionate about a particular activity, can help in building relationships. For example, running together could be an activity that binds a couple together; a weekly father son biking trip could be cherished over a long period of time. These are enjoyable activities that people look forward to doing together, which helps in strengthening social relationships.

Vis Medicatrix Naturae

Translated as 'the healing power of nature,' *'vis medicatrix naturae'* traditionally referred to the inherent healing power of the body to restore good health. A new meaning was attached to it by Professor J. Arthur Thomson in his keynote address to the British Medical Association in the year 1914. According to his interpretation, *vis medicatrix naturae* meant the healing capability of the body associated with the animate as well as inanimate components of our external environment. Many research studies conducted over the years have postulated the same conclusions—nature has a tremendous positive impact on physical as well as mental health.

It is important here to acknowledge that working out indoors has its own benefits, too, and provides a lot of flexibility. A regular trail runner, or even someone who prefers outdoor running on the streets may not be able to indulge in his or her favorite activity during the rainy season. A swimmer may not be able to go out for a swim in a natural location in case of sub-zero temperatures during winters. During these times, the option of going to an indoor setup, such as a fitness studio may be a good option. Apart from providing a viable alternative, this variation may act as a good change that may be indulged in during normal days as well. At the end of the day, it is all about incorporating an enjoyable physical activity as part of an active lifestyle.

CHAPTER TWO

Active Lifestyle

An active lifestyle is essentially a way of living in which physical activities and healthy dietary choices are integrated into everyday routines. It is a mindset, developing which may initially require a conscious effort; however, over a period of time, such choices become ingrained as part of lifestyle. The most advised and perhaps the easiest example of a step in this direction is to walk up the staircase instead of taking the elevator. It is a simple step that a person can imbibe as a lifestyle change and therefore do on a daily basis without much alteration in routine. The health benefits are immense and such a choice epitomizes an active lifestyle in the best possible manner. Not only does an active lifestyle help in preventing cardiovascular, metabolic and lifestyle diseases such as obesity and diabetes, it also greatly improves overall quality of life. A person is able to sleep better; with a positive outlook is able to work better; and is able to immensely enjoy personal, familial and social life.

Adopting a healthy lifestyle is just a few simple choices away; it does not necessarily require too many drastic changes. Yet, it is perhaps the most difficult and hardest challenge of the game. The number of people who make New Year resolutions around health & fitness goals is beyond possible count. Unfortunately, the percentage of people who are able to stick to them is an extremely small number. It takes much more than just making a resolution to adopt a healthy and active lifestyle. Small, but consistent, steps in the right direction have a much greater chance of success than large steps that may not even see daylight. By cutting out a couple of bad habits and adding a few healthy activities, a person is well on the way to a new, healthier and better life. The following section looks at areas where people can take these small steps, along with ways in which success can be achieved in this endeavor.

GETTING STARTED

As discussed above, getting started requires a lot of effort and will power to shrug off the initial inertia. It is therefore imperative that small steps be taken to initiate the process of a lifestyle change. Too drastic or too many changes can be overwhelming and can be counterproductive to the process. While most people find it difficult to get off the starting blocks, those with a lot of enthusiasm may be able to start off well. However, with too many changes, even they will find it difficult to maintain and will eventually give up. The two key words in this context are: "simple" and "consistent." The steps taken as part of an active lifestyle should be extremely simple to adopt; which means that adopting it does not require too much effort or investment, in terms of both time and money. The steps taken should be such that performing them consistently aren't too difficult. They should easily become a part of the sub-conscious so that the person does not fret about them.

- There is no need to run from home to work every day. In case the vehicle is driven down to work, it can be parked a couple of blocks away and the distance can be walked down. In case the subway is taken, then walking to and from the station could be considered.

- While going on one of the low calorie fad diets may be very appealing, it may not make too much sense. Simple steps such carrying and eating an apple everyday as part of a mid-morning snack should be considered to control the hunger pangs, rather than snacking on unhealthy and readily available pre-packaged and processed foods.

- In case there is a pet at home, taking it out for a leisurely 10-minute stroll in the morning while picking up the newspaper from the porch is an extremely simple, yet immensely pleasurable activity.

SETTING REALISTIC GOALS

In continuation with the aforementioned point, it is equally important to set realistic targets. Setting goals, which are extremely difficult to achieve, puts a lot of pressure on the individual. The first issue that arises is that the person stops enjoying the process, and starts looking at the steps taken toward the active lifestyle as a big burden. The second issue that gets built up as a result of the first one is that once an obstacle is experienced during the course, the person is inclined to give up the entire process of change itself; hence failure is imminent.

- A goal of exercising 5 to 6 days a week for 60 minutes per session may really be required for a number of individuals. Even in such cases, it is suggested to start by setting realistic and achievable goals. A more realistic approach would be to indulge in some outdoor activities such as running or biking for 3 days in the week, without any time goals. Taking out even 10 minutes from a busy work schedule is a step in the right direction. Gradually, these small steps can be built upon, and the bar can be raised.

KEEPING THE BODY IN MOTION

There are at least half a dozen simple ways in which one can keep the body moving. Initially, a push may be required in this direction, but in due course, there is an alteration in the mindset itself. Mind and body become equally inclined toward choosing options that involve movement and activity. This gets manifested in the form of pleasure and joy experienced in choosing the healthier option.

- As stated earlier, the easiest one that comes to mind immediately is taking the stairs instead of the escalator or the elevator. Stairs are encountered at a number of places. Not only can taking stairs be made a habit at workplace, but also at places such as movie theaters and shopping malls. Quite often, added benefits such as saving on waiting time for the elevator can be seen. Health issues or simply lack of fitness may be a hindrance; hence it is necessary to take it slowly and steadily. If the office is on the tenth floor, there is no need to climb the entire way on day one; it is advisable to start off with a couple of floors and gradually build upon it.

- Walking is one of the best forms of exercise that can act as filler physical activity throughout the day. Someone who complains of shortage of time for exercising may find it impossible to take out 30 minutes every day; but ten minutes accrued three times a day still adds up to half an hour of exercise. Walking down to the superstore rather than ordering over the phone, throwing trash accumulating on the desk in the first dustbin outside office rather than waiting for the housekeeping staff to clear it, walking down to the farmers' market to procure fresh produce, rather than depending on local stores that stock fruits and vegetables; the list can go on and on.

- Other ways in which physical activity and movement can be achieved is by participating and engaging in domestic activities such as cleaning the yard, and maintaining the garden. If some thought is put into choosing the activity, it can gradually develop into a hobby that is enjoyed and cherished.

CHOOSE THINGS THAT BRING JOY

Each and every one has some activity that they enjoy doing. In most cases, when a person trying to get into an active lifestyle tries naming such an activity, it is something that they have not been doing for quite a while. Whether it is walking, running or biking, none of them are time bound and therefore they don't have a minimum investment that is required. Each of them can be indulged in as part of daily life for even ten minutes. An activity that someone is passionate about and enjoys doing will be something that the person looks forward to during the day. The probability of it becoming part of the person's lifestyle is much greater than something that is force-fully done with an end objective in mind.

- Someone who enjoys biking can consider going to work a couple of days in a week. This can be done in case the distance is manageable; it can even become a routine activity if all of the elements such as shower facilities are available and conducive for utilization.

- If adventurous activities such as rock climbing and kayaking sound attractive then alternate weekends can be a starting point for such activities. In fact, becoming part of a bigger group that meets on weekdays or even making it a family affair can multiply the joy.

SIGNING UP FOR AN EVENT

For some people, a clear and precise goal acts like a good motivator. If this is the case, setting up a long-term goal such as registering for a 10k run can help define a timeline. However, it is important to break down the end goal into realistic and manageable short-term goals. A goal that is too far in the horizon can be easily pushed back in the priority order and eventually be kicked out completely. Starting off with a target of completing 2k and then extending it to 5k over a comfortable duration of 4 to 6 months (highly variable from person to person) is suggested. Using the SMART goal acronym allows individuals to have a specific, measurable, attainable, realistic and time bound goal. Other event examples include: Stand Up Paddle boarding races (short course), 20k cycling events like Bike the Bay in San Diego, California, team events like Muddy Buddy or Triathlons.

COVERING ALL ASPECTS OF LIFE

An active lifestyle is not only about performing physical exercise on a regular basis. While physical activity is the key element of an active lifestyle, but taking care of other aspects of health is equally important. There are a number of ways in which a person can take care of diet and nutrition and mental health throughout the day.

- Using fresh ingredients for preparing meals, choosing fruits and salads over processed and packaged foods for snacking for at least two days in a week, using whole grains instead of refined flour, are a few simple, non-intrusive ways in which an active lifestyle can be embraced. For almost everything that is eaten, there is a substitute, which may be healthier and at times even much better tasting. Shopping and stocking up on such substitutes and using them once or twice a week is another good option that can be explored.

- It is believed that stress is a primary contributor toward lifestyle diseases. Unless experienced first-hand, one cannot believe the impact of taking out ten minutes for meditating or deep breathing. Add onto the experience the sweet smell of nature by performing these activities out in the park or a garden near home or even work. Such relaxing activities can do wonders for overall health and general well-being, as well as improve work productivity throughout the day. Even sleeping peacefully without an alarm for eight hours a day can bring about similar benefits.

As discussed above, there are a number of ways in which an active lifestyle can be imbibed. Additional actions such as getting a partner in the endeavor, becoming a part of a group with members having similar goals, keeping a tab of things and choices made in an activity log; all help in maintaining the active lifestyle. More importantly, the person starts enjoying this new way of life.

CHAPTER THREE

Technology Available to Monitor Your Active Lifestyle

Exercising regularly, eating healthy and nutritious food and losing weight, rank amongst the top New Year's resolutions across the world. Whether it is about training for completing a marathon, or just about maintaining an active and healthy lifestyle; for most people it involves much more than just decision making and sticking to it. Tracking and monitoring progress of a newly adopted lifestyle may not be necessary for people who are extremely motivated and have a high level of patience and self-control. Unfortunately, this is not the case for a high percentage of the population.

In most cases, people get motivated when they see results. In the case of life-style changes, a lot of effort needs to be put in, and it takes quite a bit of time to see visible changes. As a result, most people quit an exercise routine or a diet plan without giving it much of a chance to succeed. The general feeling is that there is a lot of sacrifice that is being made without an iota of positive outcome. In an ideal situation, a person adopting an active lifestyle enjoys the process and therefore is not bothered too much with the results. In due course, making healthier choices is bound to show positive changes; only the amount of time to see them varies from person to person. This is where keeping a log and tracking performance and progress helps an individual in maintaining the new lifestyle that has been adopted. In addition, there are myriad other benefits that are derived as a result of such a practice.

MOTIVATION

The most important benefit of maintaining and tracking performance is motivation. When a person is maintains a log, staying on track is easier when one looks back at the efforts that have gone in over the past months and the results that have been achieved. For a person who is looking to lose weight, there can be no greater motivation than seeing a continuous decline on the graph. For someone who is looking to finish a 10k run within a certain cutoff time, seeing progress in the form of shaving off of a couple of seconds every second run, acts like a big motivator. These logs act as visual cues that remind a person that a number of small steps gradually build up to show significant achievements. At times when a person feels dejected with recent outcomes, he or she just needs to look up into the log and see the actual performance and the significant progress that has been made over the course of the program adopted as part of the new active lifestyle. All of this is based on the firm belief that an active lifestyle is bound to lead to better health and improved performance, both at work and life in general.

PLANNING

By recording and tracking the performance metrics, a person has all of the available data that is required for program analysis. Consider a person aiming to gain 5 kg of lean muscle. There are two ways in which tracking and monitoring helps in improving program effectiveness. By doing a regular body composition analysis, a person exactly knows how he or she is progressing through the workout and diet plan. It clearly tells whether the general advance is in the correct direction. Things are moving forward in case the person is gradually increasing lean muscle tissue; however, if fat percentage is increasing then intervention and program modification becomes necessary. Secondly, by logging in all of the data with regard to adherence to the workout, diet and lifestyle, it is possible to analyze in a better manner, what worked well and what did not work too well. Hence, it provides more information on how the person reached where he or she is on the current day. In the above example, during the weeks when a workout was performed in the morning, weight gain was observed, while there was lean muscle tissue loss when workouts were planned for evenings. These are clear indications of what worked well and what did not. The necessary changes and modifications can then be planned. However, in case the results are satisfactory, it is up to the individual to make a few cursory changes or to maintain status quo. Better planning increases the likelihood of the end objectives of the program being achieved.

ACCOUNTABILITY

Specific details with regard to an active lifestyle that have been written down draw a greater sense of accountability than do vague goals that have been framed in the mind. For someone looking to cut down body fat, a properly designed workout program and a calorie counted and balanced nutrition plan is of utmost importance. Open ended and subjective steps such as "cutting down on junk food" and "exercising regularly" do not work too well. However, in case these same goals are objectively written and categorically stated and maintained in a record or log, it makes a person accountable to it. Adopting an active lifestyle has to be a self-inspired change; it cannot be forced upon a person. Therefore, the only accountability is toward the individual self. A person, who planned to go paddling three times a week, may believe that at the end of the month the goal may have been achieved. In reality though, the individual may only have done an average of one paddle a week. Tracking and keeping a proper physical record helps in active lifestyle maintenance since it increases accountability.

CONSISTENCY

As repeatedly mentioned in the previous sections, consistency is the key to an active lifestyle. It is not about doing a couple of things for a limited amount of time; it is about a lifestyle change, essentially a way of life. None of the goals and objectives that a person may have in mind with regard to health and fitness can be achieved overnight. At the same time, results are guaranteed when the right choices are made and the right activities are consistently performed over a long period of time. The key to success is by taking small steps on a consistent basis. It is easy to forget the larger picture in the day-to-day hustle and bustle of life. This is where tracking and monitoring activities helps in bringing to reality the self-image that has been visualized. While writing down in a physical journal or log has been practiced over the years, technological advancement has brought forth numerous gadgets and applications that have made the process of behavioral change easier, efficient and much more effective.

There are more than a thousand gadgets, applications and programs in the health monitoring and tracking domain, that hit the market each year. The space has been in a state of constant flux over the past decade, but in the last couple of years, the pace seems to have accelerated significantly. Improved technology, better sensors and a reduction in cost of production has led to an inundation of health devices and gadgets. In addition to this, each year sees hundreds of start-ups entering the market with their versions of innovative software applications. Existing business models have been changing and are becoming more consumer oriented and output aligned. This has been due to technological changes in mobile computing, next generation networks and data analytics, further fuelled by Government impetus in areas such as healthcare service delivery and insurance.

Due to the intense activity observed in this domain, it is difficult to zero in on the device or application that is most suitable. Each and every individual has specific requirements, which need to be addressed while making choices. The following section looks at some of the popular applications and gadgets that are currently available in the market.

GADGETS
Fitbit

Fitbit is an unobtrusive activity tracker, just about the size of a small USB thumb drive. This small tracker can be kept in the pocket or clipped onto clothing. It ideally should be worn somewhere around the torso region for accurate measurement. The device is sensitive to movement and is therefore able to track the total number of steps one takes during the course of the day. In addition, it can be worn with an armband while sleeping at night and in this way, keeps track of the number of hours of sleep that a person gets.

The Fitbit software is available for Windows PCs, Macs, Android devices and iOS devices. Moreover, it is extremely simple to learn and operate. The user's activity is displayed using a personal analytics module, which is then linked to the Fitbit account. A user can view activity levels in the form of graphs depicting the number of calories burned during the day, intake of food and the amount of calories consumed; it is also possible to add additional health parameters such as fasting, blood glucose and blood pressure levels. The other aspect of the device that is extremely useful is its capability to synchronize wirelessly. A tiny receiver that gets plugged into the USB port of the computer comes as an attachment. Whenever the Fitbit is close to the receiver it transmits all the data wirelessly without the need for any manual synchronizing or physical docking. The device can also be synchronized with phones using Bluetooth. Despite possessing the capability of operating in such an inconspicuous manner, it still needs to be charged manually. However, the battery life of the device is really good, and it can be used for a full week before the requirement of charging again arises.

Fitbit is pretty decently priced in comparison to other such gadgets available in the market. Considering its user friendly attributes, it has become one of the most popular health tracking devices being used by people trying to adopt and maintain an active lifestyle.

Digifit

There are numerous health and fitness related GPS applications available for Apple products. Within this category, Digifit is a combination of an electronic attachment with a corresponding application that adds a new dimension to the so-called "i-environment." The Digifit Connect sensor is a light and compact device that can be attached to iPhones, iPad and iPod for wireless communication with other external devices such as heart rate monitors, foot pods for running and cycling power sensors. In addition, the device connects using its sensor technology to a number of different applications. These include iCardio, iBiker, iRunner, iSpinner and iPower. While some of these applications are sport specific, the Digifit and iCardio applications can be used for a number of different outdoor activities for tracking heart rate, calories being burned during a workout session, mapping and tracking sessions etc. There are a number of customization options that can be made use of; by entering data such as height, weight, sex, age etc., the device is able to accurately calculate parameters such as number of calories expended.

The applications make use of built in GPS navigation capabilities of the main device for measurement of distance and speed and for location mapping features. However, these applications still function with devices that do not have GPS capability; in such cases information such as speed and distance cannot be recorded. During workout sessions, the application can provide clues in relation to performance through vibrations, voice announcements and push notifications. All kinds of prompts and data updates can be customized according to the user's requirements. For example, a runner may program the application to provide prompts whenever the heart rate goes beyond 160 beats per minute, indicating to him or her that the pace needs to be brought down. At the end of the workout session, the application provides a complete summary that is typical of all such fitness applications.

Digifit is a versatile and inexpensive option that is an extremely attractive option for tracking, capturing and monitoring fitness related data wirelessly. The cost depends on the various mix and match options that are chosen along with the basic device. It is a good option for both indoor and outdoor activities. However, when being used in an outdoor environment for any kind of activity, care needs to be taken to protect the main gadget (iPhone/iPad/iPod) from rain and water, along with other physical hazards that generally accompany fitness activities.

Nike Fuelband

Nike Fuelband is the company's attempt toward leveraging its brand name to successfully enter and capture the fitness and health tracking space. It is a wearable health-tracking device that is in the form of a bracelet that measures the day-to-day activity level. This is done through a parameter called NikeFuel—the more active a person is during the day, greater is the amount of "NikeFuel" accrued. The device makes use of a three-axis accelerometer that measures motion, and based upon physical parameters such as weight and height that can be fed into the system, it estimates the total number of steps taken during the day, total distance covered and the total calories expended. Unlike other running specific devices, it does not provide an accurate distance measure through GPS tracking. It is also not very accurate for training purposes. However, the gadget is ideal for casual users who are looking for increasing their general activity level during the course of the day.

Daily targets can be set for NikeFuel to be amassed during the day; the device has a row of 20 LEDs that display the progress achieved toward this end. Activities that do not involve significant arm movements such as weight lifting, cycling and performing squats are not tracked very well. The device is only water resistant and not water-proof, hence it can be used in the shower but cannot be used while swimming. These are major drawbacks, since for a number of people these activities contribute heavily toward their daily activity measure. However, as mentioned above, the goal of the gadget is to help individuals monitor and increase their general activity level during the day. Toward this end, Nike Fuelband performs its task quite effectively.

The Nike Fuelband can be used in conjunction with applications developed for iPhones and other Apple gadgets. Synchronizing with the Nike+ Fuelband application is an extremely simple process; once the pairing through Bluetooth has been done, pressing and holding the device button automatically updates the application with the latest data. Cutting out features such as continuous time display and GPS has made the battery life of Nike Fuelband pretty decent, and it can last for around four to five days on a single charge. Overall, it is a device that works toward a specific goal; while it may not be useful for training purposes, it is extremely useful as a motivator for increasing activity level as part of a lifestyle change.

In addition to these gadgets, there a number of other devices such as *Jawbone UP, BodyMedia FIT* and Basis, to name just a few. Each of them has certain unique characteristics that make it ideal for a certain segment of the population. For example, Basis has different types of sensors for monitoring different parameters. The accelerometer helps in tracking sleep patterns, the optical scanner tracks blood flow and consequently heart rate; it also includes a perspiration monitor, ambient temperature and skin temperature monitors for measuring workout intensity. Some devices also possess the capability to automatically adjust to daily patterns of the user. They work in a non-intrusive manner in the background, suggesting and introducing goals and targets that can be met by the user. As technology improves, newer devices are bound to be produced each year that help individuals to track and monitor newly adopted active lifestyle for successful adherence.

APPLICATIONS

While gadgets and devices are dependent on technological advancements, application development in the health and fitness domain is taking place at a rapid pace within the bounds of existing technologies. As a result, choosing the right application to suit an individual's needs can be an extremely time consuming, and at times, a very frustrating process. The following section looks at some of the good applications that meet the requirements of different segments of the population.

MyFitnessPal

This particular application is targeted toward individuals looking to lose weight, which comprises, by far the largest segment. This free application helps in tracking activity through an activity log, and food intake through a food diary. It has a large database of food items with their nutrient composition that helps in tracking macronutrient ratios as well as micronutrient balance of diet. It has an extremely simple and customer friendly user interface, that provides important information such as calorie intake throughout the day in a very easy manner. It also provides the user with flexibility to input customized foods and recipes, which can then be accessed in future from of the database. It is a pretty simple, yet powerful application that is very popular; apart from the myriad features, this popularity may also be because it is available free of cost.

RunKeeper

As the name suggests, RunKeeper is an application that is primarily for individuals who engage in regular cardiovascular activities such as running and jogging. It has tracking, and monitoring as well as analyzing capabilities, making it an extremely popular application. It makes use of the GPS capability of the phone, and hence is useful even for other activities such as cycling, hiking and walking. As a planning tool, it allows the user to set short term as well as long-term goals and offers many features such as comparison of activity statistics, voice coaching and customization of training plans. It is an ideal application for the runners' community.

Lift

Lift is an interesting application that goes beyond just fitness and health related goals. Whether the goal is to lose weight and get back in shape or it is to become more productive at work, Lift can help the user to achieve all these goals. The application breaks down the long-term objective into smaller and manageable short term goals, increasing the chances of success. It enables the user to keep track of these so-called micro habits; it even shares it publically so that encouragement and motivation can be received from friends, family as well as acquaintances. Habits cannot only be created in this application, they can even be joined; thus, people can actually progress together on similar paths toward similar goals.

Retrofit

Retrofit is also an application that targets people aspiring to lose weight. However, its method of functioning is quite different from *MyFitnessPal*. This application gathers and helps analyze information from wireless weighing scales, Fitbit and other such devices. What makes Retrofit different is the integral usage of Skype sessions with personal trainers, registered dieticians and wellness coaches to monitor and guide the lifestyle change program. Users are able to achieve small and manageable weight loss goals (in the order of one pound of fat per week) under the guidance of experts. The application collects data from all these sources and presents it in the form of understandable and usable information.

MapMyFitness

MapMyFitness was one of the earliest applications developed in this domain. It allows users engaged in running, hiking and cycling to access its huge database that contains information on international routes, events, and listings apart from the generic fitness and nutrition calculators. MapMyFitness is not in fact a single entity, but is a collection of applications and websites. Powered by Google Maps, it provides real time data on courses and routes; information on directions, weather, elevation and traffic is readily available. The additional capability of sharing and comparing performance over specific courses with friends and participants of local fitness clubs is an interesting feature.

People have started spending much more time on applications than on the Internet browser; this is a very pertinent fact in the context. With newer technologies being developed on almost a continuous basis, gadgets and devices with improved capabilities are expected to be released in the market. However, all of these devices and application can only help in easing the process of change; the drive has to ultimately come from within the person.

CHAPTER FOUR

Physical Fitness Components as They Relate to Outdoor Pursuit Activities

There are at least 8 different components of physical fitness that need to be targeted while designing any workout program. It is practically not possible to incorporate workouts for each of these components in each session; neither do exercises exist that cover all the components simultaneously. However, it is crucial to address each of these components at least 2 to 3 times on a weekly basis. The different components, along with examples, have been explained below.

1. Muscular Strength—The force that muscles generate against a resistance (e.g. holding or stopping an object or person).

2. Power—The ability of the muscles to exert maximum force instantly in an explosive burst of movements. It has two components—strength and speed (e.g. jumping or a sprint start).

3. Agility—The ability to perform continuous explosive power movements quickly in opposing directions (e.g. zigzag running).

4. Balance—The ability to control the position of the body either stationary (e.g. a handstand) or while moving (e.g. a gymnastics stunt).

5. Flexibility—The ability of muscles to achieve an extended range of motion around a joint (e.g. performing a leg split).

6. Muscular Endurance—A muscle's ability to perform continuous work (e.g. legs for cycling or biceps for doing biceps curl continuously).

7. Cardiovascular Endurance—The heart's ability to deliver blood to working muscles and their ability to use it (e.g. running long distances).

8. Co-ordination—The ability to perform the above listed components together so that effective movements can be achieved.

In this particular context, one of the big advantages of outdoor activities is that they cover multiple aspects of physical fitness in one single workout. For example, while cycling is known to be an extremely good cardiovascular activity, it also helps in improving muscular endurance, especially the quadriceps or the front portion of the thighs. In addition, large muscle groups and multiple muscles are exercised since most activities involve compound muscle movements.

We shall now begin analyzing in detail the most important components of physical fitness in relation to outdoor pursuits.

CARDIOVASCULAR ENDURANCE

The most important requirement of the body is that of oxygen. For any living tissue to sustain itself and perform its function adequately, presence of oxygen is a prerequisite. For performing any kind of exercise, different muscles of the body need to contract and during this process of contraction, the oxygen requirement goes up. The oxygen delivery and utilization mechanism is called the cardiovascular system and the ability of the body to perform this function efficiently is called *cardiovascular endurance*. When the process of respiration is also included for study, the system is referred to as the cardio-respiratory system or cardiopulmonary system. These systems consist of the following elements:

- *Cardio*—The term refers to the heart, which is the main pump of the body. It is responsible for sending oxygen rich blood to different parts of the body and receiving de-oxygenated blood from the different parts.

- *Pulmonary*—The terms refers to the lungs. This organ is responsible for inhaling oxygen from the atmosphere and exhaling carbon dioxide into it. It is also the site where these gases are either mixed or extracted from blood.

- *Arteries*—These are blood vessels that are responsible for carrying blood away from the heart.

- *Veins*—These are blood vessels that are responsible for carrying blood to the heart.

- *Capillaries*—These are extremely thin blood vessels that branch throughout different tissues in the body and are the site for exchange of nutrients and gases that are carried by the blood.

How does the cardiovascular system function?

To understand the concept of cardiovascular endurance in a better manner, it is first important to get a hold on the functioning of the system itself. The basic step–wise functioning of the cardiovascular system has been described in brief below:

1. Carbon dioxide is extracted from the deoxygenated blood by the lungs and exhaled into the atmosphere. At the same time, oxygen that has been inhaled from the atmosphere is used for enriching this blood.

2. Oxygenated blood is carried by the pulmonary vein from the lungs to the heart.

3. The heart then pumps this oxygen rich blood to the different parts of the body using the major artery called the aorta and its branches.

4. The capillaries then extract oxygen from the blood that has been brought from the heart by the arteries and transfer this oxygen for utilization to the working muscles.

5. The muscles use up this oxygen for contraction and release carbon dioxide as a by-product. The capillaries are again responsible for taking this carbon dioxide and passing it to the veins.

6. The veins are the blood vessels that carry the deoxygenated blood back to the heart. The heart then pumps back this carbon dioxide rich blood back to the lungs using the pulmonary artery.

7. Finally, the lungs extract the carbon dioxide from this blood and enrich it with oxygen that has been inhaled as part of the respiratory process.

When all of the elements in the system are functioning well, there will be proper supply and utilization of oxygen by the tissues and the body will be able to function efficiently.

What is Cardiovascular Fitness and How is it Beneficial?

Cardiovascular fitness, or *cardiovascular endurance,* is therefore the ability of the lungs and heart to supply oxygen rich blood to the different parts of the body through the vascular system, and also the ability of the muscles to take up this oxygen and utilize it. It is important to note here that cardiovascular endurance refers to both the ability to supply, as well as the efficiency of utilization. Contrary to popular opinion, the inability of the respiratory system to inhale oxygen more rapidly (even though this appears to be the case, as a result of heaviness of breathing experienced) does not stop a person from exercising at high intensities; it is the inability of the exercising muscles to utilize the oxygen available that leads to reduction in workout intensity and subsequent termination.

Improvement in cardiovascular fitness can be achieved by regular and sustained physical activity. A number of chronic adaptations take place in the body as a result of regular physical activity. Physiological parameters such as stroke volume, heart rate, cardiac output, sub-maximal and maximal oxygen consumption, all undergo change in a manner that the overall performance of the cardiovascular system improves. Not only does the capability of the body to perform physical exercises at higher intensities improve; even at rest, the demands placed on the heart for oxygen delivery reduces, since the body becomes more efficient in utilizing the available oxygen. Moreover, a healthy cardiovascular system helps in preventing numerous life threatening diseases. These include myocardial ischemia or heart attack, coronary artery disease, congestive heart failure, peripheral artery disease, stroke and hypertension. Indirectly too, cardiovascular fitness helps in preventing lifestyle diseases such as obesity, metabolic syndrome and diabetes.

What are Cardiovascular Fitness Activities?

In common parlance, cardiovascular exercises or cardio activities refer to all of those physical activities that involve rhythmic and repetitive motion of large muscle groups of the body. Outdoor cardio activities include running, trail running, jogging, hiking, brisk walking, cycling, swimming, rowing and skiing. Most sports such as basketball, rugby, soccer, football and hockey, involve considerable amount of running and hence help in increasing cardiovascular fitness. Even during winters, when the external weather conditions and outdoor environment may not permit outdoor sports such as cycling and soccer, there are a number of outdoor activities that are still more engaging, interesting and beneficial than exercising indoors. These include snowboarding, cross country skiing, ice skating, ice hockey, curling and ice climbing. These activities require some amount of technical training, but once the basic skills have been imbibed, they have a significant, positive impact on cardiovascular fitness.

Performing cardio activities requires muscular contraction to take place on a continuous basis, which in turn requires production of sufficient amount of energy. The muscles of the body can contract in such a continuous manner when energy is produced continuously from the metabolism of carbohydrates and fats stored in the body. This continuity can be maintained only when the process takes place in the presence of oxygen. The imposed demand for oxygen as a result of performing cardio exercises leads to increased work being done by the cardiovascular system. Like all of the other muscles in the body, the cardiovascular system, too, adapts itself when it is subjected to greater demands. It is surprising to know that even a small amount of cardio activity can lead to significant health improvements. In fact, the greatest relative improvements are actually seen in the most unfit segment of the population. Fifteen to twenty minutes of cardio activity performed 3 times a week is a good starting point for absolute beginners. Gradually as the body adapts to these demands, the intensity can be increased to keep the process of improvement going.

MUSCULAR STRENGTH

Muscular strength, as described in the previous section, is the total amount of force that the body can exert against an external resistance. In real terms, it refers to the body strength that helps in performing activities such as lifting a heavy load, pushing or pulling a vehicle in case of breakdown, defending ground while playing rugby or football etc. Improving muscular strength also helps in preventing injuries that may occur while performing chores that make use of weaker muscle groups.

Muscular strength can be further classified into: 1.) Dynamic and 2.) Static strength. Dynamic strength is related to the force being generated by a particular muscle while performing a particular movement. It is expressed in terms of 1 Repetition Maximum or 1RM, which means the maximum amount of weight that the body can lift for 1 repetition. Performing a pull-up in an overhang climbing route that does not offer footholds, also involves utilization of muscular strength. Static strength, on the other hand, is the amount of force that can be exerted against an immovable object. Isometric exercises that require considerable force generation such as forearm plank fall under this category. Measurement of static strength is a tedious and expensive proposition.

Importance of Developing Muscular Strength

Each and every individual, including women, children and older adults need different muscles in their body to possess strength. Most physical activities performed during the course of the day require muscular strength. Whether it is to climb stairs, lift an infant, open a jar or carry groceries, all of these activities require a generation of force and consequently need muscular strength. In case of muscle weaknesses, the individual is unable to perform these tasks; the bigger issue is that such weaknesses make the person susceptible to injuries. Inadvertently lifting a heavy load or twisting suddenly may lead to serious injury that may take a lot of time to heal. One of the most common problems observed in recent times is chronic back pain. Weakness in core body muscles—both abdominal and back muscles, is the main reason behind lower back pain. Weak rotator cuff muscles lead to shoulder injuries while weak leg muscles—quadriceps and hamstring contribute to knee problems. Strengthening all of these major muscle groups on a regular basis—at least 2 to 3 times a week can considerably reduce chances of such injuries.

Starting from the age of 35 to 40 years onward, each and every individual starts losing lean muscle tissue and consequently muscular strength. In addition, it is also believed that muscle function also declines with age; which means that muscles tend to generate lesser force as age progresses. In middle-aged adults, this loss of strength leads to acute as well as chronic aches, pains and injuries. The problem is more serious in older adults, where weak muscles may result in falls while performing simple activities of daily life; these can be extremely dangerous and even fatal at times. Exercising for improving muscular strength can at least slow down, if not completely reverse these age related muscle atrophy issues.

Maintaining muscular strength by performing outdoor exercises that targets this component of physical fitness can abate the signs and symptoms of many diseases. A few of these benefits include—prevention of bone mineral loss that may lead to osteoporosis, improvement in blood glucose control for diabetics, reduction in pain and weakness for people with arthritis. Other benefits of indulging in outdoor strength training exercises include improved sleep, better mood, an increase in metabolic rate that helps in maintaining an ideal weight and overall better physique that improves self-confidence and self-image.

Outdoor Workouts for Muscular Strength Development

According to the Physical Activity Guidelines released for adults, strength-training exercises directed toward increasing muscular strength of all large muscle groups should at least be performed twice a week. While the option of lifting weights performing isolated exercises in a gym jumps into most minds, the functional effectiveness of these exercises to develop muscular strength is very limited. Rarely do we make use of only a single muscle to perform a particular movement; invariably multiple muscles as well as multiple muscle groups are utilized for a task. For example, lifting a heavy weight like a sack of rice correctly, makes use of the muscles in the legs as well as those of the lower back to a certain extent. Therefore, by performing strength training exercises for single isolated muscles will not improve muscular strength and coordination for doing such work. Even the best of personal trainers, having realized and experienced first-hand this particular fact, are gradually switching over to functional training exercises even in gyms and fitness centers. Functional training equipment simulating outdoor exercises have become an integral part of all indoor setups as well. As can be expected, the real thing has to be better than a simulation and therefore, outdoor workouts for muscular strength training are preferable.

The exercises that can be included as part of outdoor workouts can be classified into one of the categories mentioned below. These exercises can be combined in different ways to increase the overall effectiveness of the workout. For example, while isometric exercises and calisthenics can be performed individually with appropriate rest between sets; a variation called circuit training (involves back-to-back performance of multiple exercises targeting different, without pause; period of rest only after completion of full circuit) can be an extremely effective alternative.

Calisthenics

Calisthenics refers to exercises that consist of simple rhythmical movements that are performed without any equipment or apparatus. They make use of body weight as the external resistance and help in increasing muscular strength. Movements include a combination of actions, such as jumping, kicking, bending, pulling, twisting and swinging. These exercises are often performed in conjunction with stretches that improve flexibility and when these exercises are performed vigorously they also contribute towards cardiovascular fitness and muscular endurance.

- **Upper body exercises**—Push-ups, incline push-ups, pull-ups, over-grip and under-grip chin-ups, parallel bar dips or chest dips, triceps dips.

- **Lower body and core exercises**—Sit-ups, crunches, squats, full squats, single leg squats, lunges, split leg lunges, calf raises.

- **Compound movement exercises**—Burpees, jumping jacks, mountain climbers, jump squats, and jump lunges.

Isometric Exercises

Isometric exercises are exercises that involve only static muscle contractions. In simple terms, this means that there is no change in length of the muscle and hence, there is no movement that takes place. Pushing an immovable object such as a stationary wall is an isometric exercise since there is no movement that takes place. They are intense exercises that can help in building lean muscle as well as in burning fat. They are often used for rehabilitation after an injury for increasing the muscle strength.

Isometric exercise can be classified as either being maximal or sub-maximal exercises. The previous example of pushing an immovable object and pushing against a wall while in a wall squat position, are maximal muscle actions. These exercises induce hypertrophy or lean muscle growth and help in increasing muscular strength. Sub-maximal isometric exercises are those that involve only a sub-maximal muscle action and hence do not significantly contribute to muscle growth. Examples include lifting a weight and holding it in that position, holding a yoga pose and performing a forearm plank.

Plyometrics

Commonly known as *jump training,* plyometrics are types of exercises that help in increasing power and muscular strength. Usual strength training exercises involve slow, controlled movements; plyometrics on the other hand, involve fast, explosive movements that aim to increase speed and power. They were originally developed for athletes but have now become a part of workouts for people of all ages. These exercises are beneficial to muscle fibers, tendons and the nervous system as well.

There are three distinct phases in any plyometric exercise. First, there is a rapid lengthening of the muscle (also called eccentric movement); the second phase is a short rest period or pause, which is called the amortization phase; finally, there is an explosive movement caused by muscle contraction (also called the concentric phase). The three phases comprise one repetition, and the cycles need to be performed as rapidly as possible. It is believed that by reducing the time duration between the eccentric and concentric phases, speed and strength both can be improved. The logic behind plyometric exercise is that, when the muscle is stretched, some energy is lost as heat but energy also gets stored in the elastic components of muscles. This energy can be made use of in the subsequent contraction; however, it is only utilizable if the contraction happens immediately after the stretch. The whole process, also known as the stretch shortening cycle is the mechanism behind plyometric exercise.

These exercises are extremely intense in nature and put a lot of load on the muscle fibers and tendons. Therefore, it is important the individual taking part in plyometrics eases into the program in a gradual manner. In the initial phase, the focus should only be on form and technique, so that the exercises are performed in a safe and controlled manner. Examples of plyometric exercises include lateral jumps, squat jumps, power skipping, tuck jumps, box jumps, alternate leg bounding, vertical depth jumps, and plyometric push-ups.

Other Workouts

There are quite a few different accessories that introduce variations in different exercises that have been discussed above. *Resistance band workouts* help in increasing muscle strength of some muscles that may need extra attention or development. These resistance bands are available in different resistance options, and as muscular strength increases greater resistance can be applied for the same exercises. Another new and extremely popular training technique that has recently hit the market is *TRX Suspension Training*. It is a trademark system that makes use of straps that can be hung over walls and outdoor elements such as garden swings and trees. Workouts can then be performed by either holding the straps with hands or by suspending feet by inserting them into the straps. For example, push-ups and forearm planks can be performed by suspending feet in the straps in a manner that the upper body then becomes almost parallel to the ground. TRX is a portable system that can be easily used in outdoor settings to introduce variations in a number of muscle strengthening exercises.

Outdoor Sports Activities for Muscle Strengthening

High intensity sports activities such as kayaking, stand-up paddle boarding and rock climbing help in building muscular strength as well as endurance. A boxer practicing with a punching bag requires tremendous muscular strength, both of the arms and that of the core for performing the practice drills. A rock climber needs to have extremely strong legs, arms and specially *latissimus dorsi* muscles that are required for holding a hand-hold while pushing with the legs upward. Regular practice leads to tremendous strength gains especially of these muscles. Most of the other sports as well are include a combination of repetitive movements that help in improving muscular strength, along with other components of physical fitness as well.

MUSCULAR ENDURANCE

Muscular endurance is the ability of the body to perform a sub-maximal effort task over a period of time. This translates into performing a task repeatedly, such as lifting a weight and keeping it down again and again. It is also the measure of sub-maximal effort in terms of holding time while performing isometric exercises; holding a weight with arms extended for a considerable amount of time, tests the muscular endurance of the different muscle groups involved in performing this task. Unlike muscular strength, muscular endurance tests the capacity of muscle fibers to perform work over a longer duration of time rather than at a particular instant.

Muscular endurance is important for performing a number of tasks and for many sports activities that involve repeated movements of the same muscles. The best examples of activities that require tremendous muscular endurance are hiking, outdoor running, stand-up paddle boarding, cycling and cross country skiing.

Before we go further, it is important to reiterate the fact that almost all activities involve different physical fitness components; the percentages may vary significantly. This means that while cross-outdoor running involves muscular endurance it also requires cardiovascular endurance, balance, agility and coordination. All facets of physical fitness are therefore crucial for optimal health and performance.

Now, once the requisite muscle strength exists to perform a particular task, further improvement in performance will depend on muscular endurance. The reason why fatigue develops is that, due to limited conditioning of the muscles being used, energy production mechanism functions in a manner that it leads to build up of lactic acid. This causes a burning sensation that eventually leads to termination of the activity. Without getting into too many details, it can be understood that by improving muscular endurance, not only does the system become more efficient at producing energy to sustain activity for prolonged periods of time; it also prevents premature fatiguing by becoming efficient at getting rid of waste products such as lactic acid, that are produced during energy production processes and subsequently hamper sustained activity.

Training for Muscular Endurance

Training for muscular endurance involves doing tasks or actions that require sub-maximal force production on a continuous basis. Increased enzyme activity that helps in continuous and efficient production of energy, increased energy production capacity of cells in tissues, increased density of capillaries making the nutrient and gas exchange process more efficient, and coordination and efficiency in muscle fiber recruitment; these are some of the positive changes that happen as a result of muscular endurance training. This eventually results in an increased capacity to perform endurance activities.

The principle of specificity is also important in this current context. While all kinds of outdoor activities such as biking, trail running, hiking and paddling help in improving muscular endurance; they do not do so equally for all movements and all muscles. Therefore, while biking may lead to better muscular endurance of the lower body (calf and quadriceps muscles), rowing helps improve muscular endurance of the arms and core body. Also, the muscles used for running are slightly different from those used for biking; hence, while training for running, will help in improving overall lower body endurance, it will be much more effective in improving endurance of muscles that are specifically recruited for running. Performing body-weighted exercises such as pull-ups and push-ups also helps in improving muscular endurance of the specific muscles involved in these exercises. Circuit training that involves performing a sequence of different exercises without rest, also is an effective method of improving whole body muscular endurance.

Endurance is crucial for training and practicing for improving performance since repetitive action also leads to improvement in skill level. Doing this requires a lot of stamina, which builds up by training specifically for muscular endurance. Hence, this aspect of physical fitness is extremely crucial for work as well as sports performance.

FLEXIBILITY

Flexibility is the range of motion or movement about a joint or a group of joints; it is also referred to as "pain free range of motion." It is one of the most neglected components of physical fitness that becomes more and more important as age progresses. Runners pay attention to their running drills, cyclists perform exercises for increasing their muscular strength and endurance; in both of these outdoor activities the priorities are very clear. Often these participants concentrate only on the components of physical fitness that show direct improvement in performance. Quite often there is paucity of time and flexibility training is what gets left out. While flexibility does not depict direct obvious performance benefits except in the case of individuals participating in activities such as gymnastics, high jump, hurdling; stretching exercises that improve flexibility indirectly enhance performance in endurance related activities.

A barbell that is seen in the gym needs to be extremely strong to withstand the tremendous weight that lifters load onto it. It seems obvious that this bar should be made up of the purest and the hardest iron that is available. Reality is quite the contrary; a small percentage of aluminum, which is a softer metal, is added to the iron to increase flexibility. This addition reduces brittleness, which drastically brings down the probability of breakage. As can be seen, flexibility is adding onto the strength component in terms of functionality. The human body seems to be no different in this regard. Quite often, people say that they are innately tight and inflexible. While genetics seem to contribute to the natural ability of a person to flex, like all of the other components of physical fitness, even flexibility can be improved significantly by working on it on a regular basis. Therefore, it is important to incorporate flexibility training as part of regular exercise. If possible, stretching can be done after all workout sessions. Even if this is not done, each muscle group should at least be stretched twice a week.

Specificity of Flexibility

Flexibility is muscle and joint specific. This means that an individual who may have flexible shoulders need not necessarily have a flexible lower back. Someone with a loose upper body may have extremely tight hamstring muscles in the legs. As can be deduced from this observation, a person performing flexibility training exercises for the shoulder joint will not end up having flexible hamstring muscles. However, in general, people who take care of flexibility training do it for their whole body and therefore the flexibility of the entire body improves as a result.

The other aspect of specificity is that it is movement specific. An individual who is able to do front splits in an easy manner, may not be able to perform side splits with the same amount of ease. Even though in both these cases, movement occurs at the hip joint, the muscles being stretched are different. Therefore, flexibility for doing these two actions is different; hence, flexibility is said to be movement specific.

Benefits of Flexibility

When flexibility training is done on a regular basis, the chances of injury during sports activities, especially those that require agility, go down drastically. In addition, even those injuries that may occur while performing certain activities of daily life, such as picking up a heavy laundry basket or raising an infant up in the air, are prevented. The underlying reason is that flexibility makes the muscles pliable and decreases the resistance of connective tissues. Hence, chances of crossing the range of motion limit and consequently injury get limited; tissue damage is prevented as a result of this. A parallel example is that of a rubber band. A brand new rubber band is pliable and extensible. Stretch it by about 20% and upon releasing it comes back to its natural length. Now, take an old rubber band that has been lying in a cupboard shelf for more than a year. Stretching it by 20% may lead to breakage as a result of low pliability and extensibility. The same concept is more or less applicable to our muscles, tendons and joints.

Chronic low back pain is one of the more widespread issues experienced by people across the world. Improper posture and a sedentary lifestyle that incorporates numerous working hours in front of a desktop are the primary reasons that can be linked to this problem. Absence of any form of flexibility training leads to tight muscles of the back, abdomen, hip flexors and hamstring. This accentuates the problem. Regular stretching along with core strengthening helps in improving posture and body balance. In addition to this, proper alignment of connective tissues takes place which means that the muscles of the body are much more relaxed, helping to maintain proper posture.

Numerous research studies have confirmed additional benefits that are derived from regular flexibility training. These include improved blood flow to tissues, better dispersion of lactic acid after exercise, reduction in post-exercise soreness experienced in muscles and enhanced muscle coordination. While there are many schools of thought that dispute these claims, the direct benefits of pliable and flexible muscles cannot be denied. By regular flexibility training, one can get rid of all the aches and niggles that seem to suddenly occur while performing even the simplest of domestic chores.

Outdoor activities that improve flexibility

Stretching forms the basis of any training program that aims to improve flexibility. Most activities make use of flexibility, whether static (holding a part of the body at full range of motion, as in a pose held while performing gymnastics) or dynamic (usage of full range of motion when a fast action is performed but not held, as in the case an athlete arching his or her back while doing a high jump). However, to improve flexibility, it is important that stretching exercises be performed on a regular basis to gradually increase range of motion about a joint. There are different modes of flexibility training that can be performed in outdoor settings. In fact, indulging in any of these activities in a park or garden or even any isolated location away from noise, can be one of the most calming and peaceful activities of the day. Whether an individual enjoys activities like running, hiking or paddling a fifteen minute period in an open and fresh environment dedicated to improving flexibility, can have immense physical as well as mental health benefits. A few of the ways in which flexibility training can be performed in outdoor settings have been discussed in brief in the following section.

Stretching

There are different techniques of stretching, each of them being unique in the way in which they are performed as well as uniquely suited to the specific training objectives. A brief description has been provided below.

- *Static stretching* – This stretching method involves performing a movement at a particular joint and taking it as far as possible, as long as there is a slight discomfort but certainly no pain. The stretch is then held for a small period of 10 to 30 seconds. The stretch is then performed for a few more repetitions. It must be ensured that undue stress is not placed on the muscle while performing this stretch. Static stretches performed individually are called active stretches, while those performed with the assistance of a partner are called passive stretches. These stretches are slow and controlled and therefore can be easily performed by people of all ages and fitness levels.

- *Dynamic stretching* – In this method of stretching, dynamic movements are performed through the full range of motion. For example, while stretching the limbs, in dynamic stretching, arms and legs are moved gradually increasing speed and reach. Like static stretching, these are also controlled stretches and do not involve any jerks or bouncing movements. Typical examples of dynamic stretches are leg swings, arm swings and torso twists. These are the usual exercises that are performed by athletes as part of warm-up before indulging in sports activities, and mimic the movements that are required to be performed during the main activity itself. Since these stretches involve movement, there is a chance that small traumas may occur in case the stretch is not performed correctly; it is therefore important to learn the technique properly or perform it under supervision of an expert.

- *Ballistic stretching* – Ballistic stretching is essentially dynamic stretching that involves bouncing movements. The aim is to reach the end of the range of motion and then to use momentum to force the stretch slightly beyond the range of motion. Once this is done, the body pulls itself back into the normal range, pretty similar to the way in which a spring works. A simple example of ballistic stretching is to take up a wide stance and bending down in fast bouncing movements in an attempt to touch the toes. Since this form of stretching involves uncontrolled movements there are chances of injury. Recent studies have also questioned the effectiveness of this form of stretching, since it does not allow the muscle to adjust itself to the stretched position. Some research studies have in fact stated that these stretches may be counterproductive to improving flexibility.

- *PNF Stretching* – Proprioceptive Neuromuscular Facilitation Stretching – This form of stretching originated in and was used predominantly in clinical settings for rehabilitation purposes. Of late though, this stretching technique has been adopted by athletes as well as general population and is considered to be the most effective form. PNF techniques need to be performed in assistance of a partner and involve a combination of contraction followed by passive stretching. There are three common PNF stretching techniques, Hold–Relax PNF technique, Contract–Relax PNF technique and Hold–Relax with opposite muscle contraction technique.

Dancing

Dancing is an activity that is enjoyed by people across all age groups. While it is a good physical activity by itself, the health benefits derived get magnified when performed in an outdoor environment which is rich in oxygen. Flexibility improves as a result of movements such as swinging, twirling, twisting and dipping that are commonly used in dance steps. Group classes that involve vigorous dance movements have become quite famous in recent times. Not only do they improve cardiovascular endurance, they also help in increasing flexibility.

Swimming & Paddling

Activities such as swimming and paddling not only help in improving cardiovascular endurance and muscular endurance, they involve stretching movements and hence improve flexibility as well. Most strokes that are performed in swimming involve full stretches of arms and legs for moving forward in water. Freestyle, butterfly and back strokes stretch the elbow and shoulder joints; while the flutter kicks stretch out the joints in the legs. Swimming a couple of times a week, can build up overall flexibility of the body apart from improving other aspects of physical fitness.

Yoga

Yoga has been practiced for thousands of years in India, and of late westernized yoga classes that concentrate on certain aspects of *yoga*, especially *asanas* or physical poses have become extremely popular. These physical poses resemble static stretches and help in improving muscle tone and also lengthen the muscles. Greater freedom of movement, increased relaxation and improved overall flexibility are the benefits of yoga. There are numerous versions of yoga that have become quite popular in recent times. Breathing techniques and meditation are integral components of yoga and therefore, sessions performed in an open, calm and peaceful environment close to nature, brings out the best in this form of exercise & relaxation. A caveat here is that while performing yoga is in general safe since movements are slow and controlled; a number of poses require proper technique and form, and therefore learning them from an expert prior to performing them is advisable.

Pilates

Pilates is a form of exercise that concentrates on using the core muscles, yet builds strength as well as flexibility throughout the body including arms, legs, back and abdominals. The emphasis is on alignment of the spine and pelvic, breathing and developing a strong core to improve posture, balance and coordination. The system itself is extremely flexible, allowing different exercises to be modified to alter the range of difficulty to suit beginners as well as advanced exercisers. Intensity can then be gradually increased over a period of time to increase impact. While performing Pilates on a regular basis leads to stronger and well sculpted abdominals, it lengthens muscles, reduces muscle tension and improves joint mobility. Again, like most other forms of exercise discussed in this section, it is best when Pilates is performed outdoors; the main reason is that it involves deep breathing and there is no better environment to do this than in an external natural environment that is rich in fresh air.

Flexibility is an extremely important component of fitness and should be given due importance. Each exercise program should have a section dedicated towards flexibility training. Not only does this improve performance in sports activities but also helps in performing activities of daily life in an efficient manner, even as age progresses.

ENERGY SYSTEMS IN THE HUMAN BODY

To design an optimal outdoor workout suited to individual goals and needs, it is necessary to follow a few basic concepts of exercise science. To perform any activity energy production is a prerequisite and therefore the first and foremost concept is that of energy systems – how does our body produce and utilize energy?

Energy is present in various forms in the universe; however, in the context of the human body there are four main forms that are important. Plants convert solar energy into chemical energy which is stored in food. We as human beings consume food and convert the chemical energy into a few different forms – heat energy to keep the body at a constant temperature of 98.6°F, electrical energy for sending nerve impulses to and from the brain to different body parts, and mechanical energy for movement and locomotion. In this particular section we shall strive to understand the manner which the human body produces, stores and utilizes energy. Subsequently we shall also delve into the way in which we can train the body to make it more efficient in utilizing energy to perform different outdoor activities.

BASICS OF ENERGY PRODUCTION MECHANISM

The food that we consume is a combination of macro-nutrients – carbohydrates, fats and proteins; these are primary energy molecules that are utilized for production of energy. The process of digestion is responsible for breaking down or metabolizing these energy dense compounds and converting them into simpler usable compounds. These compounds include glucose and glycogen, which along with fat are either present in the bloodstream or are stored at different sites in the body. The body then converts all these compounds into Adenosine Tri Phosphate (ATP) whenever energy is required for doing work. This ATP is the only compound that the body can use for energy production. Hence, all other compounds mentioned above must be necessarily converted into ATP for energy production purposes.

Some amount of ATP is stored in the muscles which can provide energy for 2 to 3 seconds of muscle contraction. Whenever the body needs energy, it uses the stored ATP first, and then starts the process of tapping into the reserves for production of new ATP for sustaining work. The rate at which fresh ATP can be produced determines the amount of work that can be performed as well as the work rate. Understanding this process of replenishment and utilization of ATP is the crux of energy systems.

DIFFERENT COMPOUNDS USED FOR ENERGY PRODUCTION

As discussed in the previous section, the body makes use of different compounds for manufacturing ATP, which is then utilized for energy production. The demand rate at which energy is required along with availability, determines which compound shall be chosen for producing ATP and consequently energy. The table below shows all the major sources of energy in the body. It roughly captures the number of calories that can be produced from each source; however, as can be expected, these figures vary greatly from one individual to another. The measure of distance has also been captured to give an idea of the amount of work that can be performed using each of these sources.

Energy Source	Storage Form	Total Calories	Distance covered *
ATP	Muscle Tissues	1 to 1.5	18 yards
CP	Muscle Tissues	4 to 6	80 yards
Carbohydrates	Glucose (Blood)	20 to 22	325 yards
	Glycogen (Liver)	400 to 430	4 to 5 miles
	Glycogen (Muscle)	1,500 to 1,700	18 to 20 miles
Fat	Free Fatty Acids (Blood)	9	130 yards
	Triglycerides (Blood)	85	0.9 to 1 mile
	Triglycerides (Muscle)	2,800	32 miles
	Adipose Triglyceride	90,000 to 1,25,000	950 miles
Protein	Muscle	37,000	350 miles

The work rate has been assumed to be constant at 100 calories per mile

To summarize the table, carbohydrates are stored in the body in the form of glucose in blood and glycogen in liver and muscles. Fats are stored in the form of triglycerides and free fatty acids in the blood; and in the form of triglycerides in the fat tissues or adipose. Protein which is present in the muscle tissues rarely gets used of production of energy. Another important fact is that it is also possible to convert one energy compound into another. For example, the excess carbohydrate that is ingested gets converted into fat and is then stored in the body. During prolonged bouts of exercise, proteins may also be converted in carbohydrates of production of energy.

WHAT IS THE NEED FOR DIFFERENT TYPES OF ENERGY COMPOUNDS?

The body requires all these different energy compounds since different amounts of energy at different rates are required for performing various tasks. To understand this, let us consider the case of our prehistoric ancestors. In the dangerous environment that they were living in, rapid energy production was required to flee from imminent danger such as when there was an attack from carnivorous animals. As a result of this requirement, adaptation took place and the body became efficient at producing the requisite energy at a rapid rate. Then there were also times of food scarcity, when the body had to go without food for long periods. The body had to adapt to these conditions and depend upon internal stored reserves for surviving. It gradually led to the body becoming efficient at storage, being able to maintain buffers of molecules that provided large amounts of energy. Since both these requirements existed simultaneously, the body developed capability to meet both these demands efficiently by being able to utilize different compounds at different times.

Take the case of various outdoor sports. Each sporting activity requires a different amount of energy. Further, the energy is also required to be produced at different rates. A sprinter such as Usain Bolt, who runs 100 meters, requires a sudden burst of intense energy but only for a very short period of time, perhaps, not more than 10 to 12 seconds. On the other end of the spectrum there are long distance marathoners such as Haile Gebrselassie who require large quantities of energy over a prolonged period of time, but at a much lower rate. The physical requirements posed are extremely different in both the sports, and therefore different sources need to be tapped into for energy production. In-built genetic make-up along with training adaptations, make the sprinter's body more adept at performing explosive and fast paced activities, while the long distance runner's body is more tuned towards producing energy at a slow rate but for long periods of time. However, both of them are capable of performing the other's activity but perhaps not as efficiently. That is why Haile Gebrselassie can sprint 100 meters but will not be able to beet Usain Bolt at it. To put all this in a nutshell, different energy compounds such as ATP, carbohydrates, fats etc. produce different amounts of energy and at different rates. These biochemical reactions that lead to production of energy form the basis of all energy systems in the human body.

ENERGY PRODUCTION SYSTEMS

There are three pathways through which energy production takes place using these energy compounds. These pathways differ in terms of the energy substrate used for production of energy, in terms of whether they occur in the presence or absence of oxygen and in terms of the rate at which they produce energy.

1. *ATP – CP System*. This system uses ATP and Creatine Phosphate present in the muscles for production of energy. This system can function in even in the absence of oxygen hence it is anaerobic in nature. This system can be used for production of energy only for a few seconds irrespective of the intensity of exercise. ATP provides energy for the first 3 to 4 seconds and CP is utilized for the subsequent 5 to 7 seconds. The ATP – CP system is made use of for high intensity activities such as sprinting and overhang climbing moves that last for a maximum of 10 to 12 seconds. In case energy is required for a longer duration then other pathways need to be relied upon for the purpose.

2. *Anaerobic system or Lactic Acid system*. In case high intensity activities need to be performed for durations greater than 10 to 15 seconds then anaerobic system comes into picture. Anaerobic means that the system works in the absence of oxygen; glucose in the bloodstream

and glycogen in the muscles are the primary fuels used for production of energy. This system is used for activities such as 400 meter runs that take place at near maximal intensities. This system can produce energy at a rapid rate but can only last for 30 to 100 seconds.

3. *Aerobic system or oxidative system.* Aerobic systems are capable of producing the largest amounts of energy but can do so at very low rates. Presence of adequate amount of oxygen is a prerequisite hence this system can only be utilized for activities that are performed at lower intensities. It is important to note here that the term aerobic means 'in the presence of oxygen'; it should not be confused with aerobics, which is a popular form of group exercise that aims at improving cardiovascular endurance and burning excess body fat. Unlike the anaerobic system, this oxidative system can use a variety of energy substrates for producing energy. These include glycogen stored in the liver and muscles, triglycerides, free fatty acids and even protein. Initially when the intensity of exercise is slightly high, carbohydrates are used for energy production. This may last for 3 to 4 miles and for some elite athletes up to 15 miles; however, when all the carbohydrate sources get depleted, fat becomes the predominant energy substrate that is used for production of energy. Hikers, backpackers and cyclists therefore depend on aerobic breakdown of fat since they require large amounts of energy for extremely long durations.

Switching from aerobic to anaerobic energy system

We have been discussing intensity of exercise in the above section, stating that anaerobic system is used for high intensity activities while energy is produced aerobically for activities that are lower in intensity. The term *anaerobic threshold* needs to be understood in this context.

The aerobic system is much more efficient at energy production since it produces a greater amount of ATP in comparison to anaerobic systems for the same amount of fuel. The rate of production of this energy is however quite slow. When we are at rest the basic energy requirements of the body are met through aerobic pathways only since this energy is required at a low rate. Now, let us consider the example of walking. When we start walking at a slow pace, the energy requirements of the body go up in comparison to the requirement at rest. However, this demand is small and can still be met aerobically.

As the work rate increases and we begin to jog at say 6.5 miles per hour, the aerobic system becomes incapable of providing energy at this increased rate. The intensity of exercise has increased so much that enough oxygen is not available for aerobic systems to work. At this particular stage, the body switches over to anaerobic systems for meeting the energy demands. This point of switching is called anaerobic threshold. As can be predicted, this point of switching varies from person to person, depending on fitness levels. For absolutely untrained individuals, this switch may take place at an intensity which is only 30 to 40% of their maximum capacity; for elite athletes, this switch occurs at around 80% of their maximal capacity, hence they can perform their activities at near maximal intensity for long periods of time.

Transition Between Different Energy Systems

Another important aspect to understand here is that the human body does not work in binary—only 0 and 1. What this means is that at any particular instance, energy is not obtained from only one single pathway. While all systems contribute toward energy production, the percentage of contribution varies from rest to maximal intensity. The table given below depicts this distribution.

Duration of Exercise	ATP – CP system	Anaerobic system	Aerobic system
4 to 5 sec.	96%	3%	1%
10 to 12 sec.	60%	30%	10%
1 min.	20%	55%	25%
3 min.	8%	42%	50%
6 min.	4%	26%	70%
10 min.	2%	8%	90%
30 min.	1%	3%	96%
60 min.	< 1%	< 2%	> 98%

As can be observed from the table, all three systems are utilized for production of energy at any particular instant. These percentages are only indicative, and the figures vary on the basis of fitness level of the individual.

DESIGNING CARDIOVASCULAR ENDURANCE WORKOUTS
Introduction to cardiovascular fitness training

Cardiovascular or cardio-respiratory endurance training refers to the ability to perform repetitive movements of large muscle groups at a moderate to high intensity for an extended duration of time. The aim is to increase the rate of respiration as well as heart rate such that extra physiological stress is placed on the cardiovascular system leading to positive adaptations. The imposed demand leads to improved cardiovascular endurance through enhanced oxygen delivery mechanism as well as increased capacity of the exercising muscles to use the oxygen that is delivered for energy production purposes.

GENERAL TRAINING PRINCIPLES

There are different modes of exercises that lead to improvements in cardiovascular fitness. Trail-running, cross-country skiing, paddling, hiking and cycling are examples of the best outdoor cardiovascular workouts. While all of these activities will lead to certain specific adaptations, in general all of these activities will improve cardiovascular fitness. This means that a trail runner, who runs on a fairly regular basis, will be able to improve the speed at which he or she runs. Similarly, a skier or a rower will be able to perform their activities at a greater intensity. While these improvements are specific to the activity being performed; overall general cardiovascular fitness improves in all of these activities. There are a few basic principles that are pertinent in the context of cardiovascular endurance program design.

- *Principle of Overloading*—The extra stress that is placed on the cardiovascular system by performing exercises at high intensity is called *overload*. This overload is essential to challenge the cardiovascular system so that positive adaptations may take place. The minimum amount of overload required is called threshold.

- *Principle of specificity*—According to the principle of specificity, performing particular exercises leads to adaptations that help in performing that particular activity in an improved manner. General adaptations leading to overall cardiovascular fitness occur, but only to a limited extent. While it is difficult to determine exact percentages, it is generally believed that half the positive changes take place as a result of peripheral adaptations and the remaining half due to central adaptations. To put this in simpler terms, consider the example of an SUP paddler. Paddling predominantly involves movement of the upper extremities and also uses core muscles. Regular paddling will lead to positive heart rate adaptations while paddling is done. Therefore, to get getter at SUP paddling the person must train paddling SUP.

COMPONENTS OF A CARDIO WORKOUT SESSION

Any cardiovascular exercise session should include three distinct phases—warm-up, endurance phase and cool down. Each of these phases is extremely important and has a specific role to play in the workout session.

Warm-up

Warm-up phase is the transition period from state of rest to the state of intense exercise. The purpose is to ease into the exercise session so that undue stress is not suddenly placed on the body. The exercising muscles and the cardiovascular system are prepared for the exercise session that will follow. It leads to a gradual increase in heart rate, respiratory rate, core body temperature. It reduces the susceptibility of the muscle tissue as well as connective tissue to damage and thereby increases safety of the workout session. For older adults, an extended warm-up session is advisable to prevent ischemia or lack of oxygen to the cardiac muscles that may occur in case of sudden exertion.

During this phase, the same activity that will be performed during the session, should be performed for around 10 minutes at an intensity that is much lower than the target intensity for the exercise session. For example, the warm-up phase for a running session should be a brisk walk, followed by jogging at a slow to moderate pace. Similarly, warming up for a cycling session should essentially be cycling that starts at a low intensity and progresses to moderate intensity. This session may also include some stretching exercises, though care should be taken that these stretches are performed once the body has warmed up slightly.

Endurance Phase

The endurance phase is the main part of the exercise session. Correct amount of overload above threshold during this phase promotes positive cardiovascular adaptations. Any cardiovascular endurance exercise session can be understood in terms of certain key parameters; these have been described in detail below.

Mode

The mode of exercise refers to the activity that is performed for improving cardiovascular fitness. A predominant number of outdoor activities help in improving this aspect of physical fitness. While some activities, such as trail running and hiking are body weight bearing, in other activities such as paddling and cycling body weight does not come into picture since the body is supported. The choice of exercise should depend on interest levels as long as there are no contra-indications to exercising. This means that an individual should choose an exercise form that he or she is most interested in, as long as there are no health issues (someone who has chronic knee pain should avoid running and choose activities such as swimming or kayaking that will not put undue stress on the knees). Typically, activities are classified into three groups:

- Group 1 activities are those that can be performed by maintaining a constant intensity level and do not require much skill to perform. Examples include walking and cycling. These activities can be performed at constant and controlled intensity levels and are therefore also chosen for rehabilitation purposes.

- Group 2 activities are those that can be performed at a constant intensity but require some amount of skill to perform. Examples include recreational swimming, kayaking, SUP or cross country skiing. Once the technique is mastered, it is not too difficult to perform the exercise at a steady intensity.

- Group 3 activities are those that cannot be performed at a constant intensity level and also require a good amount of skill. The energy expenditure is highly variable since intensity cannot be controlled. Examples include all kinds of outdoor activities such as ultra-runners, Iron Man/Women, long distance SUP racing. A professional athlete will be burning at least ten times more energy while racing in the Molokai to Oahu race than an individual paddling for leisure.

Whatever the form of exercise chosen, it should be ensured that it is performed with correct biomechanical form and technique. Not only will this prevent any kind of acute as well as chronic injuries, it will also lead to improved performance through positive adaptations.

Frequency

Frequency of exercise refers to the number of times the exercise should be performed during the week. For sedentary individuals, starting off on an exercise program, even 20 minutes a session and a couple of sessions in a week are sufficient. Frequency can then be increased gradually as fitness improves. Different goals may require different frequencies, but in general, for improving cardiovascular fitness exercising 3 to 4 days per week at the required intensity levels is more than sufficient. While many people who enjoy running and skiing might propound exercising all days of the week, it is certainly not advisable. The exercising muscles need good amount of rest and nutrition to recover and grow so that they can adapt to meet the increased demands that are imposed on them. In case intensity of exercise is kept at the lower end of the range, then frequency may be increased slightly.

Intensity

Intensity of exercise refers to the rate at which exercise is performed. The speed at which an individual runs, the pace at which a biker pedals, the stroke rate at which a paddler paddles; these are all representative of the intensity at which the activity is performed. The greater the intensity of the activity, the greater the overload will be that is imposed on the cardiovascular system above the threshold. There are numerous methods to determine the intensity of exercise, some of them require expensive equipment and are accurate, while others may either use inexpensive equipment for measurement or may even be estimates; even these work pretty well under normal circumstances when exact measurements are not required for professional purposes. We shall be taking up the two main methods up for discussion.

Maximal Oxygen Uptake

Exercising muscles impose an increased oxygen demand on the body. Let us denote this oxygen requirement or uptake by the term VO_2. It is measured as the volume of oxygen taken up per kilogram of body weight per minute; the units therefore are 'ml/kg/min'. The oxygen requirement at rest is therefore denoted by VO_{2rest} and the oxygen uptake at maximal intensity is denoted by VO_{2max}. For any individual, VO_{2rest} is equal to 3.5 ml/kg/min irrespective of age, sex and fitness levels; however, higher the fitness level greater will be the value of VO_{2max}. This is also referred to as 1 Metabolic Equivalent or 1 MET. Exercise intensity is commonly measured in terms of METs. Greater the MET value, higher will be the intensity of exercise. The following table shows the MET values for common activities and sports.

Intensity	MET	Activity
Rest	1.0	Complete rest
Very Light	1.3	Standing
Light	2.0	Walking at a very slow pace (1-2 miles/hr)
Moderate	3.5	Walking at a moderate pace (3 miles/hour), leisurely rowing or kayaking
Moderately Vigorous	4.5	Slow swimming, paddling leisurely, brisk walking (3.5-4 miles/hour)
	6	Jogging (4.6 miles/hour)
	6 - 7	Hiking 5 miles at 2 miles per hour
Vigorous	6 - 8	Canoeing, rowing, kayaking, (all at a high intensity)
	6-10	Cycling (15-16 miles/hour), swimming (moderate to fast), calisthenics, aerobics
	7 - 12	Hiking 10 miles at 2.5 miles per hour with a 2,000' elevation gained
	8	Jogging (5 miles/hour), cross country skiing
	10	Running (6 miles/hour)
	13.5	Running (8 miles/hour)
	16	Running (10 miles/hour)

During the exercise session, as the intensity increases, greater amount of oxygen is required for sustaining the activity and hence the oxygen uptake increases from VO_{2rest} to VO_{2max}. The capability of the body to increase the oxygen uptake is measured in terms of VO_2R or VO_2 Reserve. This VO_2R is the difference between VO_{2max} and VO_{2rest}. According to American College of Sports Medicine (ACSM), the recommended range of exercise intensity is between 40% and 85% of oxygen uptake reserve.

$$\text{Target VO}_2 \text{ (lower end of range)} = ([40\%] \times [VO_{2max} - VO_{2rest}]) + VO_{2rest}$$

$$\text{Target VO}_2 \text{ (higher end of range)} = ([85\%] \times [VO_{2max} - VO_{2rest}]) + VO_{2rest}$$

Equations for Calculating Exercise Intensity

For all of the different kinds of activities, it is possible to measure the value of VO_2 for a particular intensity. By measuring VO_{2max} of the individual, it is then possible to work out the intensity at which exercise needs to be performed.

Walking

$$VO_2 \text{ (ml/kg/min)} = [(0.1 \times S) + (1.8 \times S \times G) + 3.5] \text{ (ml/kg/min)}$$

Here, S is the speed of walking in meters/minute and G is the percentage gradient expressed as a fraction. Once we know the individual's VO_{2max} then we can calculate the range in which the person should exercise. The speed and gradient of exercise can then be decided on the basis of this VO_2 range.

Running

$$VO_2 \text{ (ml/kg/min)} = [(0.2 \times S) + (0.9 \times S \times G) + 3.5] \text{ (ml/kg/min)}$$

Here, S is the speed of running in meters/minute and G is the percentage gradient expressed as a fraction.

Cycling

$$VO_2 \text{ (ml/kg/min)} = [(1.8 \times WR)/BM + 3.5 + 3.5] \text{ (ml/kg/min)}$$

Here, WR is the work rate measured in kg x meter/minute; and BM is body mass in kilograms. Some bikes come with attachments that can measure the work rate; it can also be calculated by measuring the crank size and resistance offered (in case of stationary bikes).

Stepping

$$VO_2 \, (ml/kg/min) = [(0.2 \times F) + 1.33 \times 1.8 \times H \times F + 3.5] \, (ml/kg/min)$$

Here, F is the frequency of stepping in minutes; H is the height of the step in meters.

There are a few issues that are encountered when this method is used to define the intensity range in which the activity should be performed.

- Measuring VO_{2max} requires a complicated and expensive apparatus. Without the value of this measure, it is impossible to determine the intensity range.

- This method is a measure of the intensity of the activity, and does not take into account the individual's response to exercise. Therefore, in case physiological response parameters such as heart rate are not measured, it can be dangerous. For example, while running outdoors at a particular speed, the oxygen uptake is constant; however, under extremely hot and humid conditions, the response of the body is very different. Therefore, while it may be fine to run at 8 miles/hour in a moderate environment, it may not be suggested in case the weather is very hot and humid, since it will lead to a higher than normal heart rate and body temperature. This method makes no such distinction.

Heart Rate

Using heart rate to decide intensity of exercise is one of the most practical and popular methods. It represents the individual's response to exercise and can be easily measured. The heart rate can be easily monitored while exercising and modifications in the intensity can be made so that the level of exertion remains under control. When heart rate is used to determine exercise intensity, the maximum heart rate of the individual represented by

HR_{max} needs to be known. There are two ways to determine this—first, it can be measured by doing a maximal test (this requires laboratory settings for testing); second, an age predicted estimate (220 - Age) can be used for the purpose. The prescribed intensity of exercise should be such that the heart rate is between 64% and 94% of maximum heart rate.

Target HR (lower end of range) = $[HR_{max}]$ x 64%

Target HR (upper end of range) = $[HR_{max}]$ x 94%

As an example, consider the case of a 20-year-old healthy adult, who wants to start an exercise program. The estimate maximum heart rate will be (220 – 20 = 200) beats per minute. The range of heart rate should be between (64% x 200 = 128) beats per minute and (94% x 200 = 188) beats per minute. During exercise, the heart rate should remain between 128 and 188 beats per minute. For healthy adults, the higher end of the range can be used; therefore exercise intensity should be such that the heart rate remains around 150 to 170 beats per minute. For unfit and deconditioned individuals, the lower end of the range should be used; hence heart rate should be around 130 to 150 beats per minute.

A better method to determine this range is the Karvonen method. Oxygen consumption and heart rate are directly proportional; when one increases the other increases linearly and vice versa. Therefore, the same methodology applied for oxygen consumption can be used in this context as well. Unlike VO_{2rest}, which remains constant for all individuals, HR_{rest} needs to be measured for each person. Greater the fitness level of the individual, lower will be HR_{rest} since there will be a lesser load on the heart to pump.

Target HR (lower end of range) = $([40\%] \times [HR_{max} – HR_{rest}]) + HR_{rest}$

Target HR (higher end of range) = $([85\%] \times [HR_{max} – HR_{rest}]) + HR_{rest}$

In the same example of the 20 year old, if the HR_{rest} is 75 beats per minute, then the range is 125 to 181 beats per minute. This result corroborates with the previous method used for calculation. In exactly the same manner, the range can be narrowed down depending on the age and fitness level of the individual.

Unlike the case of oxygen uptake, intensity cannot be hard coded for heart rate. There can be no formula that can be fixed for calculating intensity for running, walking, paddling or cycling on the basis of heart rate that needs to be maintained. The heart rate should be measured during the course of exercise using a heart rate monitor or by measuring directly by palpation. When the heart rate crosses the upper end of the range, intensity of exercise can be reduced; when it goes below the lower end of the range, intensity can be increased.

There are a couple of issues that are faced when heart rate is used to determine exercise intensity.

- Estimation of maximal heart rate on the basis of age is generally used for the purpose rather than doing maximal testing; this can sometimes be inaccurate. There can easily be an error of 10 to 12 beats per minute when such an estimate is used for calculations.

- Medications such as beta-blockers used by hypertensive individuals (those with high blood pressure) suppress the heart rate. This can be dangerous since other physiological parameters may be changing normally and may go beyond prescribed range.

Despite these limitations, using heart rate for prescribing and modifying workout intensity is one of the most practical and fairly accurate methods.

Rating of Perceived Exertion (RPE)

RPE is an exercise tolerance guideline used for monitoring and altering exercise intensity. On a scale from 6 to 20, the individual rates his or her level of exertion experienced (6 representing no exertion at all, and 20 representing absolute maximum). It is a simple and convenient method that can be used in all settings. It is believed that cardiovascular benefits are derived when the intensity is kept between 12 and 16 on the RPE scale. For individuals who have difficulty in determining heart rate or those who consume medication that alters heart rate, this system is useful.

Category Scale	Perceived exertion level
6	
7	Very, very light
8	
9	Very light
10	
11	Fairly light
12	
13	Somewhat hard
14	
15	Hard
16	
17	Very hard
18	
19	Very, very hard
20	

15-category scale also known as the Borg scale

Calorie Expenditure

Energy is expended whenever work in any form is performed. However, the number of calories expended in any exercise depends on the mode, intensity and duration. It is a measure that provides an overall summary of the workout. While designing a workout program, the number of calories to be expended needs to be taken into consideration. This decision itself depends on the goal of the program. Regular physical activity that leads to expenditure of around 1,500 calories per week is associated with a decrease in risk related to all-cause mortality. For purposes of weight loss, overweight and obese adults should target an expenditure of around 2,500 calories per week at the minimum. Previously sedentary and deconditioned individuals should start slowly, and gradually increase calorie expenditure by varying the different exercise parameters such as intensity, duration and frequency.

Calorie expenditure depends a lot on the skill level of the individual. However, in case of group 1 activities that can be maintained at a constant intensity, proper calorie expenditure calculations can be done.

Calories expended $= (MET \times 3.5 \times BW \times T)/200$

Here, MET is the Metabolic Equivalent of the exercise form as discussed in the section on oxygen consumption; BW is the body weight in kilograms and T is the duration of exercise in minutes.

For example, if a 150 lbs. runner runs at 7 miles per hour with 0% gradient for 45 minutes, then the number of calories will be calculated as following:

$VO_2 \ (ml/kg/min) = [(0.2 \times S) + (0.9 \times S \times G) + 3.5] \ (ml/kg/min)$

$= [(0.2 \times 190.17) + (0.9 \times 190.17 \times 0) + 3.5] \ (ml/kg/min)$

$= 41.534 \ (ml/kg/min)$

$MET = VO_2/3.5$

$= 11.87$

$Calories\ expended = (MET\ x\ 3.5\ x\ BW\ x\ T)/200$

$= (11.87\ x\ 3.5\ x\ 150/2.2\ x\ 45)/200$

$= 637\ calories$

Tracking the number of calories expended can be really useful, especially for individuals who aim to lose weight by participating in outdoor activities. However, the aforementioned calculations can be done only for activities that can be performed at constant intensity, which does not vary with skill level. A number of outdoor activities are such that it may not be possible to do these calculations. The table given below gives an idea of the calories that can be expended by an individual who has the basic skills required to perform the activity efficiently. The activities are both outdoor pursuit activities as well as active lifestyle activities. Also, additional activities were included to offer a brought perspective.

Activity	Energy Expenditure (calories/min/kg)	Activity	Energy Expenditure (calories/min/kg)
Racquetball (recreational)	0.07	Cycling (light, <10 mph)	0.12
Kayaking (leisure)	0.04	Cycling (light-moderate, 10-12 mph)	0.10
Dancing (general)	0.08	Cycling (moderate, 12.1-14 mph)	0.14
Golf (walking + bag)	0.09	Cycling (hard, 14.1-16 mph)	0.18
Running (5 mph, 12 min/mile)	0.12	Cycling (v. hard, 16.1-19 mph)	0.21
Running 5.5 mph (11 min/mile)	0.14	Cycling (stationary, 50W)	0.05
Running (6 mph, 10 min/mile)	0.16	Cycling (stationary, 100W)	0.09
Running (6.6 mph, 9 min/mile)	0.19	Cycling (stationary, 150W)	0.12
Running (7.5 mph 8 min/mile)	0.22	Cycling (stationary, 200W)	0.18
Running (8.6 mph, 7 min/mile)	0.24	Cycling (stationary, 250W)	0.22
Running (10 mph, 6 min/mile)	0.28	Calisthenics (push-ups, etc.)	0.08
Chopping Wood	0.09	Circuit Training	0.14

Mowing Lawn (walking, power)	0.08	Weight Training (light)	0.05
Raking Leaves	0.07	Weight Training (hard)	0.10
Trimming (manual)	0.07	Rowing (50W)	0.06
Weeding/ Gardening	0.07	Rowing (100W)	0.12
Sitting Activities (very light)	0.03	Rowing (150W)	0.15
Standing (very light)	0.04	Rowing (200W)	0.21
Walking (3 mph 20 min/mile)	0.06	Stretching/Yoga	0.06
Walking (3.5 mph, 17 min/ mile)	0.07	Aerobics (low impact)	0.09
Walking (4 mph 15 min/mile)	0.08	Aerobics (high impact)	0.12
Sweeping	0.05	Volleyball (recreational)	0.05
Washing Car	0.07	Running: cross-country	0.16
House Cleaning	0.06	Hiking: cross-country	0.11
Washing Dishes/ Ironing	0.04	Rock Climbing: rappelling	0.19
Cooking Food	0.04	Swimming (light)	0.10
Carrying Groceries (light)	0.07	Swimming (moderate)	0.14
Laundry Folding/Making Bed	0.04	Stand-up Paddle Boarding (moderate)	0.18

| Playing with Kids (sitting) | 0.04 | Child Care (sitting) | 0.05 |
| Playing with Kids (standing) | 0.05 | Child Care (standing) | 0.06 |

Adapted from McArdle, W., Katch, F., & Katch, V. (2001). Exercise Physiology: Energy, Nutrition, and Human Performance (5th Ed.). Philadelphia: Lippincott Williams & Wilkins.

To calculate energy expenditure, multiply the figure given in the table by the body weight of the person in kilograms and the duration in minutes. For example, a person weighing 150 lbs indulging in moderate intensity swimming for 60 minutes will expend: Calories expended = 0.14 x (150/2.2) x 60 = 573 calories

Duration

The duration of exercise session and intensity are inversely proportional to each other, as the intensity increases duration for which it can be performed decreases and vice versa. This means that high intensity exercises can be performed for shorter durations and low intensity exercises can be performed for much longer durations. According to ACSM, an aerobic activity session should last for 20 to 60 minutes; this does not include warm-up and cool down and is the measure of endurance phase only. Sedentary and deconditioned individuals should start with 20 minutes and gradually increase the duration as fitness improves.

Training Method

Once the mode, duration, intensity and frequency of exercise have been figured out, the appropriate training methodology must be chosen. Selection of a training method depends on physiological response as well as personal choice; however, using a mix of training methods as part of the exercise progression plan is advisable. Each of these methods works toward improving a certain aspect of fitness and hence should be included in some dosage. As with other parameters, even the choice of training method depends on the goals of the individual as well as his or her fitness level. There are five major training methods that are employed as part of any cardiovascular endurance-training program.

1. Continuous training—As the name suggests, this training methodology is based on maintaining a near constant intensity level. Activities include walking, running, cycling etc. which belong to group 1 and hence can be performed at a constant intensity level. For those with limited functional capacity, continuous training at around 40% of maximal capacity is suggested as part of conditioning phase. Intermediate programs lasting between 20 to 60 minutes are ideal for general fitness improvement and body fat reduction. Long duration workouts that continue for more than 60 minutes are employed for athletic training in sports such as cycling and distance running. Prolonged exercise can lead to musculoskeletal injuries, hence such long duration activities should be performed after at least 6 to 8 months of regular moderate intensity workouts.

2. Interval training—This methodology involves alternating between bouts of high intensity cardiovascular exercise and relatively low intensity ones. It can be used by beginners as well as by experienced exercisers such as professional athletes for improvement in aerobic capacity. The parameters that need to be defined for interval training programs include intensity of bouts, duration of each interval, duration of rest period and number of repetitions of bouts. Such an interval program can be both aerobic as well as anaerobic. Aerobic interval training program includes bouts of exercises that are around 60% of functional capacity, performed for 5 to 10 repetitions of 2 to 5 minutes each. The low intensity periods between bouts should last

for around 2 minutes. Anaerobic interval training is performed at a much higher intensity level, decreasing the duration of each bout; it should be performed by athletes who have a high degree of cardiovascular fitness.

3. Fartlek training—This training methodology is similar to interval training, except that the training bouts are not accurately monitored and measured. The intensity as well as duration of the bouts is determined on the basis of how comfortable the exercising individual feels. It is one of the more common forms of training that infuses a lot of variety and therefore interest in the exercise session. However, this form of exercise should be performed by individuals who have an average or an above average cardiovascular fitness level.

4. Circuit training—This methodology takes the individual through a series of different exercise stations, each being performed for a small duration with little rest between different exercises. Rest is taken once a full circuit has been completed. Traditionally this form of training has been used for muscular endurance improvements by incorporating a series of light-weight and high repetition exercises. An example of circuit training in outdoor environment is a sequence that intersperses jogging with a variety of endurance, strength as well as flexibility exercises. Pure aerobic circuit training programs in outdoor settings can consist of bouts of cardiovascular exercises such as running, jogging, stair-climbing, cycling and skipping. Each exercise can be performed for 2 to 5 minutes at 60% of functional capacity with a 10 to 15 second rest period for switching between exercises.

5. Aerobic cross training—This is a training methodology that is very individualized in nature and is a combination of all the training

methods. Each method may further be characterized by a different mode and different intensity. Combining a group of activities at different intensities is an excellent cross-training program that keeps the interest levels high. An example of this is cycling to a pool, lake or ocean swimming there for a while and then returning by cycling back again, each part of the workout lasting for around 20 minutes. Such a mode of cross training is ideal for people who are looking to maintain their fitness levels by regular active participation in exercise.

Cool Down

The cool down phase is the transition phase from high intensity cardiovascular endurance activity back to rest. This phase allows the heart rate, respiration rate, blood pressure level to gradually come down to resting levels so that the body does not have to undergo a sudden change in physiological parameters that can have a shock effect. A gradual progression also helps in preventing post exercise hypotension or low blood pressure that result in faint headedness. This happens as a result of pooling of blood in the exercising muscles especially of the lower body; this leads to a lack of blood flow back to the heart and brain. A gradual return to a normal state also helps in dissipating body heat and removal of waste products such as lactate.

The cool down period, like the warm up, can consist of the activity performed during the endurance phase but at much lower intensity level. This phase can last for around 10 to 12 minutes. However, a long duration workout session should necessarily be followed up with a longer cool down session as well.

It is important to ensure that all of these phases are present in any workout session. Not only does it increase safety, it also leads to better adaptations that manifests in the form of improved cardiovascular fitness.

CHAPTER FIVE

Designing a Muscular Strength & Endurance Program

INTRODUCTION TO A MUSCLE TRAINING PROGRAM

A training program for muscular strength as well as endurance goals has to incorporate resistance training. This resistance can be provided either by using body weight or through external sources such as weights and resistance bands. Most outdoor activities such as stand-up paddle boarding, rock climbing, etc., that do not predominantly target the cardiovascular system, help in improving both muscular strength as well as endurance. None of these activities will selectively target strength or endurance gains; exercising regularly using these modes invariably leads to both types of adaptations. Other activities, such cycling, that make uses lower extremities, help in improving muscular endurance along with improving cardiovascular fitness.

GENERAL PRINCIPLES OF RESISTANCE TRAINING

There are a few basic principles that need to be understood while starting a resistance-training program for improving muscular strength and endurance.

- *Specificity*—This principle states that adaptations will take place specific to the type of workouts that are performed. By performing exercises for the chest on a regular basis, it cannot be expected to see strength gains in the back muscles. In terms of outdoor sports activities too, strength gains will occur only when the same kind of exercises are performed. For example, an athlete trying to gain strength for his or her SUP forward stroke can perform functional training exercises that mimic the forward stroke in dry land while targeting both the arms and core muscles. Exercises such as tying one end of a resistance band to a tree and the other end to the paddle will help in this process.

- *Overload*—As in the case of cardiovascular training, in resistance training too, it is important that overload takes place; this means that the demand imposed on the exercising muscle should be greater than what it is used to and experienced during the previous session. There should be reason for adaptations in the form of strength and endurance gains to take place. To ensure that this gain happens on a continuous basis, it is important to ensure that the muscles are progressively overloaded in each session. This can be done by varying resistance-training parameters such as the weight or resistance chosen, number of repetitions and sets and rest period between different sets.

- *SAID principle*—The Specific Adaptations to Imposed Demands or the SAID principle states that the adaptation will be specific to the type of demands that are placed on the muscles. For example, if rowing is done on a regular basis, it will help in developing muscle endurance of the arms and core; the body will get better at doing this particular action on a continuous basis.

- *Progression*—Progression is the design of an exercise program that aims at providing progressive overload. Practically, the progression plan takes a rank beginner through the initial stages when lower weights are used and gradually helps in building up strength or endurance depending on fitness goals. Generally, a progression plan provides intensity level of exercise depending on the number of weeks a person has been regularly exercising. The plan is divided into three phases—initiation stage, improvement stage and maintenance stage.

- *Goal setting*—Like any other program, a resistance-training program is also goal dependent. Parameters need to be monitored and altered depending on the goals and performance of the individual during the course of the program. The three primary goals of a resistance-training program have been explained in brief. These goals need to be specific, measurable and attainable; they should also be such that interest levels of the participant are maintained during the program so that there is no drop in intensity during the program.

  - *Muscular strength*—This is the goal of the program when individuals aim to "grow stronger." Typically, the aim is to increase strength and power so that specific activities may be performed in an enhanced manner. Athletes involved in sports such as shot-put, javelin throw and power lifting aim to increase muscular strength corresponding to the functional movements involved in their respective sports. They aim to throw a heavier weight or a weight through a greater distance; or even lift a heavier weight, as in the case of weight lifting. Other sports such as rock climbing, paddling, etc. also have an eye towards increasing muscular strength, in addition to other physical fitness facets such as endurance and agility.

- *Muscular endurance*—This is the goal of the program when individuals want to increase their stamina, or their ability to perform a task in a repetitive manner over a longer duration without getting exhausted. Activities such as hiking, cycling, kayaking, stand-up paddle boarding require tremendous amount of muscular endurance. The muscles involved in the corresponding movements contract thousands of times repetitively in a period of less than half an hour. The muscles should be able utilize energy and also capable of withstanding the fatigue that develops in such activities as a result of lactic acid build-up.

- *Hypertrophy*—It refers to the increase in size and mass of muscles. Individuals who state that they want to have large biceps or want a sculpted physique are referring to hypertrophy. In physiology terminology, whenever there is an increase in size of existing muscles it is referred to as hypertrophy.

As part of goal setting, it is important to understand that none of these goals are mutually exclusive. Exercises may target one particular aspect, such as muscular strength, but that does not mean that it eliminates the chances of any kind of strength gains or that the muscle size would remain constant. On the contrary, an individual who is starting out on a program to increase muscular strength should start off by increasing endurance and emphasize on hypertrophy, before selectively targeting strength gains.

TYPES OF RESISTANCE TRAINING PROGRAMS

Traditionally, resistance-training programs have been exercise programs that are conducted in indoor settings, such as a fitness center. However, realizing the numerous benefits derived by working out in the open, individuals have started engaging in even these traditional resistance training programs outdoors. While this section has been discussed in detail under muscular strength and endurance, a brief summary with a few atypical resistance training programs have been listed below:

- *Traditional weight training*—All of the traditional weight training exercises using free weights such as dead lifts, squats, lunges etc. can all be performed in an open, outdoor environment. Numerous open-air setups are being established and are becoming popular. The training principles remain the same; just that the benefits of an open setting get added on. Weight training using machines and free weights are ideal for people who are looking at a close monitored and controlled program. The exact effort and performance can be measured and the program can be altered on the basis of short and medium term outcomes.

  Traditional weight training systems are best for people who are looking at hypertrophy as their main goal. Bodybuilders fall into this category; the stimulus that needs to be provided to the muscles of the body to force them to grow in size can only be delivered by exercises using heavy weights. In addition, people who are beginning an exercise program and have a previous medical condition that may require monitoring are better off by starting their exercise program in such a controlled environment. A caveat here is that, while fresh air and oxygen are good additions, such setups can function only in locations that have moderate and pleasant climates. If the weather conditions are not conducive, the whole thing can actually become counter-productive, negatively impacting health and fitness.

- *Body weighted training*

  - *Only body weight*—Exercises such as push-ups, squats, pull-ups, crunches, triceps dips etc. can all be performed outdoors. These exercises use body weight as the resistance against muscle contraction and help in improving strength. Variations can be introduced to increase intensity, for example, performing single leg squats is far more intense than simple squats. By altering parameters such as number of repetitions and sets, these workouts can target strength gains more than endurance gains.

  - *Accessories*—All of the body weighted exercises, as well as others such as bicep curls, triceps extension, shoulder lateral raises etc. can be performed using external resistance provided by accessories such as resistance bands and resistance tubes. These are simple and inexpensive tools that help in either providing resistance or adding resistance to body weight, thereby helping in muscular adaptations.

- *Comprehensive outdoor fitness training programs*

  - *Parkour*—It is a holistic training discipline that has become quite popular across the globe. The training principles have been derived from obstacle course training that is extensively used in military schools. The aim is to move swiftly and efficiently through an obstacle course using the ground and other surrounding elements to help propel the body forward. Movements and exercises include climbing, swinging, jumping, running, rolling, etc. which are performed while keeping the momentum high.

- *Crossfit*—It is defined as a "variety of functional movements performed at a high intensity." It is a strength and conditioning program that covers all aspects of physical fitness, including agility and balance. Typically, workout sessions are short in duration (around 20 minutes) and high in intensity. The workout sessions include movements such as sprinting, jumping, skipping and rowing; body weighted exercises like pull-ups, push-ups; compound exercises such as squats and lunges using dumbbells, barbells, medicine balls and kettle bells; and gymnastics exercises such as parallel bars and roman rings. Sometimes entire sessions or at least components of workout sessions are performed outdoors, especially when activities are performed as part of a group.

- *Outdoor activities & sports* – Outdoor activities such as hiking, rock climbing, stand-up paddle boarding, kayaking etc. help in developing muscle strength along with building up stamina and endurance. As mentioned earlier, each of these activities improves strength of the particular muscle groups that are used for performing the activity. By conducting outdoor activities such as hiking and paddling a comprehensive whole body workout can be achieved.

HOW TO DESIGN A PROGRAM

There are a number of parameters that need to be considered while designing a training program for muscular strength and endurance gains. By altering even one of these parameters, it is quite possible that the activity that was initiated to improve muscular strength, may actually work toward developing muscular endurance instead.

- *Choice of exercises*—While choosing an outdoor sport for physical fitness, interest level of the individual needs to be the primary decision parameter. Continuity in the program will only be possible if the person is self-motivated. A person interested in cycling will not participate regularly in an activity like trail running. However, once the activity has been chosen, there are a number of exercises that need to be performed, at least once or twice a week to improve performance in the main activity itself. For example, a person who loves cycling will be able to ride much better, both faster as well as longer when his or her lower body is stronger. While cycling may only lead to limited strength gains, exercises such as squats, lunges and calf raises done periodically can have profound strength and endurance gains. These gains will manifest themselves in the form of much enhanced cycling performance. Similarly, if kayaking and Stand Up Paddleboarding are regular activities, then exercises that increase arm strength and core body strength should be included as part of the workout.

- *Order of exercises*—The order of exercises that should be performed is a small parameter that should be considered for exercises for performance enhancement of main activity. Large muscle groups should be exercise before small ones, and multi-joint movements should be performed before single joint movements. An example that covers both these points is of doing pull-ups before bicep curls using resistance bands.

- *Resistance and repetitions*—The amount of resistance used for any exercise will also define the number of repetitions that can be performed. The greater the resistance, lower will be the number of repetitions and vice versa. Higher resistance with smaller number of repetitions helps in improving muscular strength, while lower resistance and consequently higher number of repetitions help in building muscular endurance. For example, when single leg squats are performed, resistance is much higher in comparison to simple squats since one single leg has to carry the whole body weight. Therefore, an individual will be able to perform only 6 to 8 repetitions in comparison to 20 to 25 repetitions that are possible for squats. Greater resistance and smaller number of repetitions in the case of single leg squats will help in gaining muscular strength. These parameters need to be decided depending on fitness goals.

- *Number of sets*—This can be roughly translated as exercise volume in the context of resistance training using outdoor activities. Higher exercise volume with moderate resistance will lead to hypertrophy and muscular endurance, while lower exercise volume with high resistance will lead to muscular strength gains.

- *Duration of rest*—Rest period between sets is associated with the energy substrate that will be used for production of energy. Smaller rest periods between bouts of activities will lead to ATP and CP being used for production of energy through anaerobic pathways. This has been observed to enhance muscular hypertrophy. Longer rest periods that will help the body recover are much better for muscular strength gains.

As can be observed, quite a few of these parameters are inter-linked to a certain degree. By altering these parameters, muscular adaptations that will take place can be altered; this is done to achieve desired goals from the program.

MUSCLES USED FOR DIFFERENT OUTDOOR ACTIVITIES

Outdoor activities such as rowing, hiking, trail running and paddle boarding involve compound muscle movements and multi-joint movements. Therefore, unlike muscle specific exercises that are performed on gym machines, these outdoor pursuits help in achieving a complete functional workout. Apart from the exercising muscles that can be directly observed, since these activities require coordination and stabilization, numerous additional muscles are worked out. For example, while stand-up paddle boarding uses upper extremities for paddling, the balance and coordination that needs to be maintained to remain afloat on the board, engages the lower body as well as core muscle groups. The various muscle groups that are engaged in performing an activity have been mentioned in the discussion on individual sports taken up in a subsequent section of this book.

CHAPTER SIX

Design of Flexibility Training Program

As discussed in a previous section, flexibility is the pain free range of motion about a joint. It is specific to a particular movement that is performed at a particular joint. Few people in the world will argue against the belief that flexibility is one of the important components of physical fitness. It is extremely crucial for optimal health and peak performance. In the current context, all of the outdoor activities can be performed much better when the body especially specific muscles that are being used, are flexible.

Flexibility training improves static flexibility, which means that static range of motion improves about a joint. This is relevant in the context of injury prevention while performing strenuous activities as well as activities of daily life. Dynamic flexibility also improves considerably and the individual involved in activities such as rock climbing and Stand Up Paddleboarding are able to perform much better as a result of greater reach due to greater range of motion and increased extensibility of muscles.

WHEN AND HOW MUCH TO STRETCH

There is continuous controversy over what is the ideal time to stretch and for how long do stretches need to be performed. What kinds of stretches are most beneficial to specific sections of the population with specific goals is another question that is debated quite often. Most experts believe that stretches can be performed before as well as after exercise. The mode of flexibility training and the goals toward which it is performed differs for both cases.

Prior to beginning the main workout, stretches can be performed; however, care must be taken that some amount of warm-up is done so that the muscles are not cold, inextensible and therefore susceptible to injury. Active stretches should be performed to decrease the stiffness of muscles that will be used in the main activity. For example, a cyclist should stretch calves and quadriceps prior to exercise. Dynamic stretching that mimics movements similar to those of the main activity may also be performed. During the exercise session, temperature of muscles increases and they become pliable. Stretching that aims to increase long-term flexibility should therefore be performed after the exercise session. Post exercise stretching has other benefits such as muscle relaxation, facilitating restoration of normal muscle length, improved blood circulation and removal of waste products. Static stretches are ideal at this stage with these objectives in mind.

While outdoor activities do improve flexibility, specific flexibility training exercises, commonly called stretching should be performed. According to ACSM guidelines, flexibility training should be done at least 2 to 3 times a week, covering all major muscle groups. Stretches should be held for a period of 10 to 30 seconds in case of static stretches, and in case of PNF techniques further 6-second contraction should be incorporated as part of each stretch. Each stretch should be repeated for 2 to 4 times. These guidelines indicate a minimum benchmark; stretching should actually be done on a daily basis, since flexibility is one component of physical fitness that can rarely be overdone.

CHAPTER SEVEN

FITT Concept

The FITT concept is an acronym for Frequency, Intensity, Time and Type. It is a method of defining parameters for different types of training. The ACSM guidelines for healthy adults have been summarized in the table given below.

	Frequency	Intensity	Time	Type
Cardiovascular Training	3 to 5 sessions per week	40%-85% of HRR or VO_2R 55%-90% of HR_{max} 12 – 16 RPE	20–60 minutes continuous, or discontinuous 10 min. bouts aggregating to 20–60 minutes	Dynamic, repetitive rhythmic movements of large muscle groups
Resistance Training	2 to 3 sessions per week	Volitional fatigue or 2 to 3 repetitions prior to it 19 – 20 RPE or 16 RPE	Sets of 3 to 20 repetitions (lower reps for strength & higher for hypertrophy & endurance)	Different exercises that target all muscle groups

Flexibility Training	Minimum – 2 to 3 sessions per week Maximum – 5 to 7 sessions per week	Stretch to feeling of slight discomfort with no pain; stretch to the end of ROM	10 to 30 second hold time, 2 to 4 repetitions per stretch	Static stretches for all major muscle groups

These are specific ACSM guidelines for healthy adults indulging in a fitness program for general health and fitness improvements. An exercise program needs to be customized for each and every individual depending on goals. All these parameters described above need to be clearly defined for any exercise program.

EXAMPLES OF EXERCISE PROGRAMS DEFINED USING FITT CONCEPT

Example 1: Traditional training program in indoor settings

Cardiovascular training

Frequency – 3 times a week

Intensity – High intensity bout - Speed of 6 miles per hour, Incline of 15%; Low intensity bout - Speed of 3 miles per hour, Incline of 5%; 10 bouts at each intensity level

Time – High intensity bout – 2 minutes; low intensity bout – 2 minutes; 40 minutes (10 bouts of 2 minutes for each intensity level)

Type – Running on a treadmill (interval training)

Resistance training

Frequency – 3 times a week

Intensity – 2 exercises each of major muscle groups (chest/shoulder/back/legs) & 1 exercise each of minor muscle groups (calf/biceps/triceps); 3 sets of 12/10/8 repetitions with increasing resistance for each set; 45 second rest between sets

Time – Total duration of workout not more than 60 minutes

Type – Combination of machine and free weight exercises

Flexibility training

Frequency – 6 times a week

Intensity – Stretch to end of range of motion such that there is discomfort but no pain; 10 repetitions for each dynamic stretch (major movements) pre-workout and 3 repetitions for each static stretch post-workout

Time –20 second hold for each static stretch

Type – Combination of active static & dynamic stretches

Example 2: An outdoor training program

Cardiovascular training
Frequency – 4 times a week
Intensity – Hiking at 3 miles per hour with the aim of gaining 1,000 feet; coming down at around 4 miles per hour (terrain dependent) on 2 days; paddling in a protected cove for 2 days; both activities to be performed at 75% HRR
Time – 60 minutes
Type – Hiking and Paddling
Resistance training
Frequency – 2 times a week
Intensity – Day 1 - 2 body weighted exercises each for hamstring, quadriceps, calf, abdomen and oblique; Day 2 - 2 body weighted exercises each for chest, shoulders, back, biceps and triceps; 3 sets of 12/10/10 repetitions; 45 second rest between sets
Time – Total duration of workout not more than 60 minutes
Type – Body–weighted exercises
Flexibility training
Frequency – 6 times a week
Intensity – Stretch to end of range of motion such that there is discomfort but no pain; 10 repetitions for each dynamic stretch (major movements) pre-workout and 3 repetitions for each static stretch post-workout
Time –20 second hold for each static stretch
Type – Combination of active static & dynamic stretches

SAMPLE WORKOUT PROGRAM FOR OUTDOOR SETTINGS

The following workout program has been designed for a middle distance runner who has been running regularly for at least 6 months and has proper running technique.

Workout Day 1

Sr. No.	Name of Exercise	Number of Sets	Number of Repetitions	Tempo	Rest
1.	Joint Rotations set	1	5	-	-
2.	Warm–up set				
	(A) Push–ups	1	6 – 10	111	30 seconds
	(B) Squats	1	12 – 15	111	30 seconds
	(C) Walk/Run	1	10 minutes	Slow (3.0 – 4.0 mph)	30 seconds
3.	Running	1	40 – 45 minutes	Moderate (6.5 to 7.0 mph)	75 seconds
4.	Cool–down set				
	(A) Walk/Run	1	5 minutes	Slow (2.5 – 3.5 mph)	30 seconds
5.	Static Stretching set	1	1	20 second hold	-

Workout Day 2

Sr. No.	Name of Exercise	Number of Sets	Number of Repetitions	Tempo	Rest
1.	Joint Rotations set	1	5	-	-
2.	Warm–up set				
	(A) Walk/Run	1	10 minutes	Slow (3.0 – 3.5 mph)	30 seconds
	(B) Push–ups	1	6 – 10	111	30 seconds
	(C) Squats	1	12 – 15	111	30 seconds
3.	Push–ups	1 – 3	10 – 15	311	45 seconds
4.	Prisoner Squat	1 – 3	10 – 15	311	45 seconds
5.	Bench Triceps Dips	1 – 3	10 – 15	311	45 seconds
6.	Sit–ups	1 – 3	10 – 15	311	45 seconds
7.	Lunges	1 – 3	10 – 15	311	45 seconds
8.	Mountain Climbers	1 – 3	10 – 15	-	45 seconds
9.	Burpees	1 – 3	10 – 15	-	45 seconds
10.	Cool–down set				
	(A) Walk/Run	1	5 minutes	Slow (2.5 – 3.5 mph)	30 seconds
11.	Static Stretching set	1	1	20 second hold	-

Workout Day 3

Sr. No.	Name of Exercise	Number of Sets	Number of Repetitions	Tempo	Rest
1.	Joint Rotations set	1	5	-	-
2.	Warm–up set				
	(A) Walk/Run	1	10 minutes	Slow (2.5 – 3.5 mph)	30 seconds
3.	Skipping	5 – 20	Maximum repetitions in 1 minute	-	60 seconds
4.	Running/ Jogging	10 – 20	Sprint for 1 minute/Jog for 2 minute	Maximum Exertion	60 seconds
5.	Cool–down set				
	(A) Walk/Run	1	5 minutes	Slow (2.5 – 3.5 mph)	30 seconds
6.	Static Stretching set	1	1	20 second hold	-

Workout Day 4

Sr. No.	Name of Exercise	Number of Sets	Number of Repetitions	Tempo	Rest
1.	Joint Rotations set	1	5	-	-
2.	Warm–up set				
	(A) Walk/Run	1	10 minutes	Slow (3.0 – 3.5 mph)	30 seconds
	(B) Push–ups	1	6 – 10	111	30 seconds
	(C) Squats	1	12 – 15	111	30 seconds
3.	Jumping Jacks	1 – 3	10 – 15	311	45 seconds
4.	Plyometric Push–ups	1 – 3	10 – 15	311	45 seconds
5.	Squat Jumps	1 – 3	10 – 15	311	45 seconds
6.	V–ups	1 – 3	10 – 15	311	45 seconds
7.	Alternate Ankle Hops	1 – 3	10 – 15	-	45 seconds
8.	Hyperextension	1 – 3	10 – 15	111	45 seconds
9.	Kick–outs	1 – 3	5 – 15	-	45 seconds
10.	Upright Bike	1	10 – 20 minutes	Moderate (HR 130 – 140 bpm)	75 seconds
11.	Cool–down set				
	(A) Walk/Run	1	5 minutes	Slow (2.5 – 3.5 mph)	30 seconds
12.	Static Stretching set	1	1	20 second hold	-

Workout Day 5

Sr. No.	Name of Exercise	Number of Sets	Number of Repetitions	Tempo	Rest
1.	Joint Rotations set	1	5	-	-
2.	Warm–up set				
	(A) Push–ups	1	6 – 10	111	30 seconds
	(B) Squats	1	12 – 15	111	30 seconds
	(C) Walk/Run	1	10 minutes	Slow (3.0 – 4.0 mph)	30 seconds
3.	Running	1	75 – 90 minutes	Moderate (6.5 to 7.0 mph)	75 seconds
4.	Cool–down set				
	(A) Walk/Run	1	5 minutes	Slow (2.5 – 3.5 mph)	30 seconds
5.	Static Stretching set	1	1	20 second hold	-

Workout Day 6

Sr. No.	Name of Exercise	Number of Sets	Number of Repetitions	Tempo	Rest
1.	Joint Rotations set	1	5	-	-
2.	Warm–up set				
	(A) Walk/Run	1	10 minutes	Slow (3.0 – 3.5 mph)	30 seconds
	(B) Push–ups	1	6 – 10	111	30 seconds
	(C) Squats	1	12 – 15	111	30 seconds
3.	Push–ups with elevated legs				
4.	Lunges				
5.	Close grip triceps push–ups				
6.	Chin–ups	1 – 3	10 – 25	111	150 seconds
7.	Air Bike				
8.	Forearm Plank (30 second hold)				
9.	Leg Raise				
10.	Box Jumps				
11.	Cool–down set				
	(A) Walk/Run	1	5 minutes	Slow (2.5 – 3.5 mph)	30 seconds
12.	Static Stretching set	1	1	20 second hold	-

* Tempo refers to the pace at which the exercise needs to be performed. "311" for a push-up means that one should go down in 3 seconds, hold there for 1 second and come back up again in 1 second.

CHAPTER EIGHT

Designing a Workout Using Outdoor Pursuit Activities

The following section looks at various outdoor activities that can be pursued for improving physical fitness and consequently overall health. Guidelines, tips and precautions that need to be taken have also been mentioned. Following them makes these activities a safe and enjoyable experience.

HIKING

Hiking is essentially an outdoor activity that involves walking in natural environments. It is good way to spend time outdoors in natural surroundings, at the same time getting necessary physical exercise. It is an end in itself and as fitness level increases, the sense of enjoyment also increases. To avid hikers, it rarely seems like an exercise that needs to be performed; it is a leisure activity that provides additional health benefits.

Since hiking trails that are chosen involve a number of ups and downs, the activity requires strong legs and an efficient cardiovascular system. In case of longer hikes, bigger backpacks need to be carried and this engages the back muscles for maintaining proper posture and body alignment. While hiking can be done once or twice a week, a number of exercises can be performed outdoors itself, to increase functional strength that helps in developing strength and stamina. Since it is a low to moderate intensity long duration activity, the exercises should be such that they help in building cardiovascular endurance and muscular endurance of the muscles involved. Individuals beginning a program that involves hiking need to follow a few guidelines.

- *Starting difficulty level*—The main parameters that should be considered while deciding a hike are speed, distance and altitude. An easy hike would be one at a speed of 2.5 miles per hour for 2-3 miles, gaining an altitude of around 1,000 feet. A difficult one would be one at 3 miles per hour for 7-8 miles gaining an altitude of around 3,000 feet. Difficulty level is very subjective, depending on the basic fitness level of the individual, altitude at which hiking is done as well as the weight of the backpack that is carried.

- *Where to hike*—While the difficulty level of the hike is being considered, the location of the hike should also be decided upon. Some people like hiking in a densely wooded trail while others prefer open locations at an altitude; when interest levels are high, hardly any fatigue is experienced. As they say, "It's all in the mind!"

- *Solo or Group activity*—Hiking may be done as part of a group, it may also be a couple's activity. Hiking for some people is akin to a meditation session and hence they prefer solitude. While some terrains and locations may be dangerous and hiking as part of a group is advisable, in most case it is completely a matter of personal choice.

- *Clothing and Footwear*—The basic underlying statement is that, one should wear what is comfortable for walking. Clothes should cover the body and be light and breathable. Sweat should evaporate so that the body can cool down. Climatic conditions should be taken into account while determining the material of clothing. Footwear is an extremely important aspect since wrong choices cannot only be unpleasant, they can be outright dangerous. Depending on the terrain, sneakers or hiking boots can be chosen. Absolutely new footwear should be avoided at all costs; they need to be broken in for a while prior to being used for a long hike.

- *Accessories*—Jackets and hats need to be carried to counter extreme temperatures and direct sunlight. For example, despite low temperatures, it is quite possible that exposure to direct sunlight may result in a sun-stroke. These things should be considered while carrying accessories for the hike.

- *Things to carry*—Other things include first aid kit, charged mobile phone, flashlight, sunscreen lotion, pocket-knife, sun glasses, foods such as nuts, fruits, granola bars etc. and adequate amount of water. Carrying other things such as books, music players and cameras is a personal choice, though the extra weight should be factored in.

- *Other precautions*—It is advisable to check the local weather forecast, just in case it may be an issue if the terrain is difficult, dangerous and inaccessible. Further, someone in the family or friend circle should be kept well informed, so that something can be done in the event of an emergency.

It is difficult, if not impossible to include hiking as an isolated activity as part of daily lifestyle. However, hiking twice a week, followed up by exercises for building lower body strength (such as squats, lunges and calf raises) and cardiovascular endurance is a complete program that is built around hiking as the main driving activity.

Hiking seems like a great cardiovascular activity; however it can also be a muscular strength and endurance activity. If you think about how many lunges you need do to get to the top of a mountain, you quickly realize the legs workout you are getting. Below you'll see a table with the muscle group targeted in a hike and a comparative exercise in the gym.

Sr. No.	Name of Muscle	Equivalent Gym Exercise
1.	Quadriceps	Lunges, Squat, Leg extension
2.	Hamstrings	Good mornings, Leg curls, Glute-ham raise, Straight leg deadlift
3.	Gluteus	Sumo deadlift, Single leg split squat, Stiff leg deadlift, Lunges

STAND-UP PADDLE BOARDING

Stand-up paddle boarding is known by a number of names such as stand-up paddle surfing, stand-up paddling and the commonly used acronym SUP. It is an activity that combines surfing and kayaking and has become one of the most rapidly growing sports in the segment that can be performed by people of all ages. In addition, it is a really good form of exercise that targets cardiovascular endurance and core muscles strengthening.

SUP is a sport in which the individual uses a paddle to propel and move forward through water in a standing position on a surf board-like board. It requires minimum amount of equipment and the best part is that it is not necessary to have waves for SUP. It can therefore be done on a river, lake and pond. It is an easy activity that has a short learning curve and even rank beginners can pick it up really fast. Like cycling, it can be done at a leisurely pace as well as at a faster pace to make it a calorie expending aerobic activity for burning fat. Apart from the core muscles it also helps in strengthening arms and legs. Further, cross training in such unstable environments leads to improved neuromuscular coordination that helps in performing other dynamic activities. The following equipments and accessories are required for SUP:

1. *Stand-up paddleboard*—The paddleboard is the most important as well as the most expensive piece of equipment required for SUP. Starting at around $1,000, paddleboards are available for thousands of dollars at the upper end of the spectrum. An expert should be consulted for choosing the paddleboard since they come in various sizes (variations in terms of length and width). The choice depends upon the weight of the paddler as well as the experience level. While experienced paddlers can go in for narrower paddleboards, beginners should choose ones that are flat and wide and therefore provide greater stability. Paddleboards are also made up of different materials such as fiberglass, plastic and EPS foam. Inflatable and soft tops are also available for beginners.

2. *Paddle*— Paddles used for SUP are slightly different and have an elbow or angle in the shaft for enhanced paddling efficiency. In general, the size of the paddle should be 6 to 8 inches taller than the individual using it. Some experts recommend a higher differential of around 10 inches.

3. *Personal Flotation Device (PFD)*—Since paddleboards used for SUP are considered by most authorities such as the U.S. Coast Guard

as vessels, it is mandatory to wear a personal flotation device when navigating through water.

4. *Proper clothing*—Choice of clothing is weather dependent; no specialized suits are required. For cold weather conditions common dry suits and wetsuits can be chosen. In case of hotter weather conditions even t-shirts and shorts are sufficient.

5. *Sun protection*—Like most other outdoor activities, to prevent adverse effect of prolonged exposure to direct sunlight, it is recommended to use sun protection such as a pair of sun glasses and appropriate sun block.

Once the required gear is in order, the following guidelines should to be followed for beginning SUP and incorporating it as part of lifestyle:

1. *Learning phase*—As mentioned earlier, SUP has a very short learning curve. The crux is to get used to balancing the paddleboard on water. It is highly advisable to take a few classes or sessions for learning the important techniques in order to avoid injuries. Paddle boarding stance, strokes and turns have technicalities that can be easily learned from an expert. Once the proper foundation is in place, a person is able to SUP in a better manner.

2. *Choosing location*—SUP does not require waves, therefore calm and still waters also suffice. Beginners should start off SUP on lakes and ponds since balance and coordination are easier to grasp in slightly more stable conditions. Gradually, difficulty level can be increased and variations can be introduced for keeping the interest levels high.

3. *SUP as part of lifestyle*—In case accessibility of appropriate location is not an issue, SUP can be done on a daily basis. It is however

recommended that SUP be one of the many components of a physical workout plan, and therefore other muscular strength, endurance and flexibility exercises should be incorporated for at least 2 to 3 days in a week.

SUP offers an excellent full body workout that has become a supplementary cross training workout for many athletes. Since it is performed outdoors, it provides wonderful views while giving the feeling of walking on water itself!

While practicing the sport of paddling whether you are kayaking, canoeing or stand up paddle-boarding, you should be using the same core muscles. Paddling is all about torso rotation instead of pulling with your arms. Below is a table that illustrates the muscle group used in paddling and exercises that target the same muscle groups and can be done in the traditional gym.

Sr. No.	Name of Muscle	Equivalent Gym Exercise
1.	Deltoids	Anterior—Front raise, Military press, Dumbbell shoulder press; Lateral—Lateral raise, Upright row; Posterior—Lying rear lateral raise, Reverse fly
2.	Rotator Cuff	Side lying external rotation, Prone lying horizontal abduction, External rotation with resistance band/cable
3.	Supraspinatus	Cable front lateral raise, Dumbbell lying lateral raise
4.	Trapezius	Barbell/Dumbbell Shrugs
5.	Pectoralis Major	Bench press, Push-ups, Incline bench press, Incline fly with dumbbell
6.	Latissimus Dorsi	Barbell pullover, Lat Pull-down, Pull-ups, Chin-ups
7.	Abdominal muscles	Crunches, Leg raise, Reverse crunch, Sit-ups, Caterpillar crunch, Oblique crunch

ROCK CLIMBING

Apart from the thrill and excitement that is an inherent part of rock climbing, it is one of the best overall anaerobic exercises that benefit both body and mind. Once seen as only an extreme adventure sport, it has now become a part of mainstream sports. The increasing interest in rock climbing has led to a rapid increase in the number of facilities being setup across the world. While outdoor rock climbing may require some amount of expertise, indoor walls have made the sport accessible to more number of people. It is an excellent alterative for exercise for fitness enthusiasts who find exercising in an indoor fitness centers or gyms insipid.

Rock climbing is a multi-dimensional sport that challenges muscular strength, endurance and flexibility of the upper body as well as the lower body and core. In addition, the high levels of concentration that need to be maintained require disciplining mental faculties, improving overall mental health. It can be done outdoors and indoors, hence it can be practiced all year round. The sport has a number of variants that can be practiced in a variety of outdoor settings, making it really interesting and enjoyable. Bouldering, deep–water soloing, top rope climbing and solo climbing are a few examples. Through different climbing protocols, rock climbing addresses different physical fitness components such as muscular strength, flexibility, muscular endurance and cardiovascular endurance. It also helps in burning a lot of calories thereby leading to weight loss and a favorable body composition. Apart from the force that needs to be generated by the arms and legs for pulling the body upward, rock climbing also helps in developing an extremely strong core. Great amount of stabilization is required for balance and coordination; this stabilization happens as a result of continuous contraction of muscles of the core. Depending on the intensity at which it is performed, it can be a cardiovascular activity that helps in burning a large number of calories. Reaching out to grab distant holds helps in improving flexibility as the muscles are dynamically stretched out. The following guidelines may be followed while beginning on a rock-climbing program.

- *Difficulty level*—Beginners should not start outdoor climbing before they have developed sufficient muscular strength and learned the requisite climbing techniques. This has to be necessarily done under the aegis of an instructor and should not be self-taught. Even indoor rock climbing walls can be used during this stage before progressing to outdoor locations.

- *Learning curve*—Climbing is not an easy activity to pick up; while the techniques may be learned quickly, it requires development of strength, which may take considerable amount of time. It is advisable to go really slow, since hard climbs may lead to injuries that may have severe adverse effects.

- *Location*—As mentioned earlier, the versatility of rock climbing opens up numerous possibilities. The sport can be practiced in mountainous terrains, canyons and gorges and even simple boulders can be made use of.

- *Gear*—Rock climbing requires specific equipment and gear such as climbing ropes, harnesses, belaying devices and climbing carabiners, spring-loaded cams and quickdraws. The rock climber needs to wear comfortable clothing like t-shirts and shorts or tracks along with proper climbing shoes. There are a number of other devices that help in either active or passive protection.

- *Fulfilling the body's needs*—Outdoor climbing causes a lot of dehydration; it therefore important to drink plenty of water to ensure that the lost fluids are replenished. It is also a prolonged activity that taps into the body's fuel reserves. It is important to replenish the energy stores by eating simple carbohydrates immediately after the climb and complex carbohydrates during the entire day post the climb. Since the session takes a heavy toll on the body, it is recommended to take the next day off from any kind of strenuous exercise, so that the body gets time to recover.

Joining a group—Like with most other sports, the interest level and enjoyment multiplies in case it is done in groups. Not only do other members of the group provide motivation, they also share useful tips and information that may be extremely useful for fellow climbers.

In case proper safety precautions are not taken, there are chances of injuries through either overuse or falls. Rock climbing is certainly a difficult and challenging sport, but the boost in self-confidence and sense of achievement upon reaching the summit is unbeatable.

While practicing the sport of rock-climbing you'll be climbing with your feet, instead of pulling with your hands. In other words the legs will be lifting your body. You will use footholds and handholds to climb up the face of the wall. As far as footwork, you'll be edging or smearing (using friction) to climb the rock; as far as handholds, you'll be using down-pressure, cling grips, pocket grips among other techniques to hold on to the face holds. At the same time, you might do several moves including: mantel, under-cling, stemming or lie-back in order to move smoothly through the face wall or crag. Below is a table that describes some of the muscles group use in rock-climbing and the equivalent exercise you might do in the traditional gym as part of your "workout."

Sr. No.	Name of Muscle	Equivalent Gym Exercise
1.	Deltoids	Anterior—Front raise, Military press, Dumbbell shoulder press; Lateral—Lateral raise, Upright row; Posterior—Lying rear lateral raise, Reverse fly
2.	Supraspinatus	Cable front lateral raise, Dumbbell lying lateral raise
3.	Forearms	Wrist curl, Reverse wrist curl (barbell, cable, dumbbell)
4.	Latissimus Dorsi	Barbell pullover, Lat Pull-down, Pull-ups, Chin-ups
5.	Quadriceps	Lunges, Squat, Leg extension
6.	Hamstrings	Good mornings, Leg curls, Glute-ham raise, Straight leg deadlift
7.	Hip flexors	Lying leg raise, Hanging leg raise, Roman chair sit-ups, Scissor kicks, Decline sit-ups
8.	Calf muscles	Standing calf raise, Donkey calf raise, Seated calf raise, Single leg calf raise

CYCLING

Cycling is the fastest and healthiest way to go from the point of origin to the destination point. With the quality of roads having improved drastically with separate lanes in most places for riders, it has become an integral component of the lifestyle of numerous urban dwellers. Increasing traffic has meant that cycling has in fact become a faster mode of transit; at the same time since it is non-polluting, it is environment friendly as well.

Cycling is a predominantly cardiovascular endurance building exercise, which also helps build muscular endurance of the lower body and core. It helps burn calories, thereby aiding in weight loss for a healthy body composition. For adults who face issues such as knee pain and back pain, it is a really good form of exercise because of its non-impact nature. Unlike sports such as rock climbing, it does not require too much technical training, and once learned it is believed that the skills cannot be unlearned. The intensity can be varied so that the workout can suit individual capacities. The following guidelines should be followed while adopting cycling as a regular physical fitness activity:

- *Beginning*—Learning how to ride a bike is not too difficult and someone who knows how to do so can be asked for help and guidance. One can even go in for a few riding class sessions. It is advisable to start slowly and to keep off roads until confidence builds up. One should do so only when biking can be done using a single-hand so that road signals can be given. Sticking to flat roads and clear locations is recommended during the learning phase.

- *Choice of bike*—The bike retailer will be able to provide advice on the frame size ideal for the individual's body structure as well as the number of gears that may be required. Bikes generally fall under one of the following three categories:

  - *Mountain bike*—These bikes are ideal for mountainous terrain and traveling off roads. They are extremely durable, but are slow on flat surfaces as a result of greater traction.

  - *Road bike*—These bikes have a lighter frame along with narrow tires. They are ideal for high speeds and climbing hills. However, they are absolutely unsuitable for taking off the roads.

  Hybrid bike—As the name suggests, they are "in-betweens" and therefore can be used on as well as off the roads. This also means that they are less efficient than mountain bikes when riding off the roads, and slower than road bikes when on the road.

- *Choice of location*—It is important to choose the location wisely since it can get dangerous when vehicles are being driven alongside at high speeds. The choice of location also depends on the kind of bike as explained above.

- *Gear and equipment*—Cycling as a sport is dependent on a number of equipment and small devices and gadgets. Helmet, lights, reflectors are required for safety purposes. A portable pump and a repair kit that includes a patch kit and spare tubes should also be carried in case of breakdown and punctures.

- *Clothing and accessories*—Cycling shorts, t-shirt, glasses, gloves should be chosen with case so that they are comfortable, at the same time these accessories should serve their purpose efficiently. In addition, there are thousands of electronic gadgets and devices that hit the market each day. While almost all of them are non-essential, quite a few of them such as GPS tracking devices and heart rate monitors can be useful for performance monitoring.

- *Nutrition*—Like other long duration endurance exercises, cycling requires regular replenishment of lost water, salts as well as glucose and glycogen reserves. It should be considered mandatory to carry a water bottle in case the ride extends for more than half an hour. Energy bars as well as complex carbohydrates should be consumed to ensure fuel replenishment in case rides extend beyond an hour.

Cycling is perhaps the only outdoor exercise form that can be easily incorporated as part of daily lifestyle. It is not necessary to take special time out specifically for exercise; one can commute to office and even use the bike for grocery shopping. The vast number of cycling forums and discussion boards that are active online is testimonial to the growing popularity of the sport.

RUNNING

Running and jogging are the primary and most popular forms of exercise, the difference between the two being that of intensity. While jogging is done at a slower pace and hence is aerobic in nature; running is faster and invariably becomes a cardiovascular exercise that crosses the anaerobic threshold. Running is predominantly a cardiovascular activity that is accessible to each and every individual since it does not require any equipment at all. Apart from a healthy heart running also helps in weight loss since it helps in burning a lot of calories. When done at the right intensity, the body can utilize the stored fat for energy production, leading to a drop in fat percentage and a favorable body composition. As a result of the stresses placed on the skeletal system, running also helps in developing bone strength and preventing osteoporosis. It is believed that running for 2 to 3 times a week for half an hour can considerably reduce the risk of cardiovascular and coronary artery diseases.

Running is not for everyone. People with knee problems should avoid impact running, especially on an incline and choose other modes of exercises until enough strengthening has been done. It is suggested for such individuals to get a clearance from the doctor prior to engaging in a running program. While running is the most basic form of exercise, some guidelines should be followed for injury prevention as well as for optimal performance.

- *Goal setting*—The first and foremost step is that of setting appropriate goals. Whether running is done for fitness, for completing a marathon, for losing weight or simply for fun, goal setting helps in monitoring and tracking performance as well as in maintaining motivation to ensure continuity of the program. Depending on current fitness levels, individuals can choose to set targets of completing 5k or 10k runs; time based goals of running continuously for an hour can also be good goals. It is not necessary to keep goals very specific as long as the process is being enjoyed. Therefore, a person who is running for fun in the woods twice a week can aim to increase fitness so that he or she is able to do it for an hour continuously.

- *Running shoes*—While it may be tempting to just use old sneakers to start running, it is not advisable at all. Ill-fitting and poorly shaped shoes are the biggest reasons for running injuries, especially foot injuries. This is such an important issue that it may make sense to get shoes professionally fitted by experts. Proper gait analysis may also be conducted wearing the chosen shoes prior to purchasing them. One can even get a fair idea by putting on the shoes under consideration and walking around in the store. Minimalist runners prefer a different kind of shoe due to the type of stride they perform. These shoes have a very "skinny" sole.

- *Clothing and accessories*—The choice of clothes is based on comfort. Simple shorts and t-shirts are appropriate. Clothes that have good wicking properties are preferable since they will help in evaporation of sweat thereby keeping the body temperature in control. Glasses and waist pouches may be used in case the need is felt.

- *Running technique*—Everyone believes that they have the perfect running technique, which has been the case since they first started running during childhood. Unfortunately, this is seldom the case. An improper technique not only hampers performance it also leads to injuries. Some of the important technical points include looking straight ahead, keeping shoulders squared and relaxed, keeping the body upright so that shoulders are just slightly ahead of the hips, bend in the arms which are kept close to the body such that they swing backwards and forwards and not sideways, and pushing the foot down through the ball.

- *Classification of runs*

  - On the basis of location, running can be classified as trail running, urban running and indoor running. Trail running refers to running done on trails generally in mountainous terrain where there are a number of ups and downs. It also requires greater neuromuscular coordination to negotiate the undulations that are present on the running surface.

  - On the basis of running event they can be classified as track running, road running, cross-country running, trail running and fell running or mountain running.

  - On the basis of distance runs can be classified into sprints, middle distance, long distance and marathons.

- *Nutrition*—Running, especially long distance, can take a heavy toll on the body. Like most other endurance activities it is important to ensure proper nutrition and hydration. Individuals often take part in competitive runs such as marathons; it is important to load up complex carbohydrates to ensure enough glycogen reserves are present in the body for the run.

Over the years, interest in running has seen very specific spurts. Currently, we are experiencing one of these spurts manifested in the number of people across ages participating in events such as half-marathons, marathons and even ultra-marathons. However, many runners especially those who are new to the sport, commit the mistake of excess. More is not always better; excessive running complemented by improper techniques leads to injuries such as shin splints, syndrome and runner's knee. It is important to consult a physician and identify the cause in case any pain in experienced. Corrective actions taken at the right time can save a lot of trouble.

FITT for Hiking

	Low intensity	Medium intensity	High intensity
Environment	Flat terrain	Elevation gain of 750 ft to 2,000 ft.	Elevation gain of 2,000 ft to 4,000 ft.
Distance	1-3 miles	3-6 miles	7-15 miles
Resistance/Weight	5-15 lbs backpack	15-35 lbs backpack	35-60 lbs backpack
Cardiovascular target	55%-65% of HRmax	65%-75% HRmax	75%-85% HRmax

FITT for SUP and kayaking

	Low intensity	Medium intensity	High intensity
Environment	Flat water	Flat and/or small waves with current	Small waves and/or current
Distance	1-3 miles	3-6 miles	7 plus miles
Cardiovascular target	55%-65% of HRmax	65%-75% HRmax	75%-85% HRmax

Fitt for Rock climbing

	Low intensity	Medium intensity	High intensity
# of climbs/routes	2-3 routes below your highest climbing level ability (Example: 5.8)	4-6 routes below your highest climbing level ability and 1-2 routes at your highest level	6-8 routes below your highest climbing level ability and 2-3 routes at your highest level

IMPORTANT TIPS:

1. The fitness professional should instruct clients to take a formal class on a new outdoor activity that the person has never done before. Even cycling, if not perform correctly can result in body injuries.

2. Recommend your client to start with low intensity outdoor activities and then increase progressively based on their fitness level and outdoor environment.

3. Enhance the fitness program by varying the outdoor activities.

4. Encourage clients to drink twice the amount of water they drink in a gym workout and to bring a nutritional snack with them.

5. Make sure that clients include stretching before and after each outdoor activity.

6. Encourage the use of technology to capture memories, document the outdoor activity and log the workout.

7. For hiking, paddling, trail running and cycling encourage the use of a heart rate monitor. Have your client keep a log of their heart rate during the outdoor activity.

CHAPTER NINE

Safety Precautions for Outdoor Workouts

While exercising outdoors, one is exposed to a variety of environmental conditions as well as variation in terrain. An unstable external environment begets uncertainties; therefore one should be adequately prepared for a proper response. The following list identifies specific hazards and ways to counter them.

1. *Medical clearance*—For most people a Physical Activity Readiness Questionnaire or PAR-Q is sufficient for screening purposes. In case there are no medical concerns, then the person can start physical exercises. However, in case there is any issue, it is advisable to seek medical clearance from a physician prior to starting the program.

2. *Wearing proper clothing and accessories*—Wearing proper gear may only seem to contribute toward increasing comfort; however, it is important from the safety perspective as well. In hot and humid conditions, wearing clothes that do not have sufficient wicking characteristics will lead to heat getting trapped since sweat is not able to evaporate and cause cooling. This may lead to a rise in body temperature and if not checked can be fatal. Accessories such as hats, sunglasses and sunscreen are crucial in case of exposure to strong direct sunlight in order to prevent an eventuality like heat stroke.

3. *Using proper equipment*—The importance of properly functioning gear cannot be overstated. If purchasing a bicycle have the bike shop do a "fit kit" before you decide on your purchase. Do the same for a paddle if you are considering purchasing a paddle for Kayaking or SUP. Improper gear can be dangerous enough to cause serious physical injury. It should be ensured that there is no compromise on quality of safety gear such as helmets for cycling and life jacket (PFD) for paddling. As a matter of habit, all the gear and equipment should be checked once prior to usage each time. Preventive maintenance further helps reduce the chances of failure, thereby reducing risks.

4. *Awareness of warning signs and symptoms*—It is crucial to be aware of and respond to different untoward physiological responses of the body toward physical exertion. In case there is any sort of pain or discomfort, it is advisable to stop immediately. Cramps, dizziness and cold sweat are examples of signs that indicate that there is something that is going wrong.

5. *Communicate the plan*—It is advisable to tell a relative or a friend about the exercise plan. In case the plan is to go for a trail run, the route and time should be communicated properly so that in case of an emergency someone knows exactly what the intended course was. Further, as far as possible sticking to the plan communicated is recommended.

6. *Carry a mobile phone*—While it may be cumbersome to carry a mobile phone in the pocket, a number of pouches and attachments are available nowadays that do not add to the discomfort in any way. Quick dial numbers should also be stored, since time may be limited in case of an emergency.

7. *Carrying identification*—Carrying identification is quite self-explanatory; it should be ensured that it contains up to date information. Apart from emergency contact numbers, other useful information such as blood group and allergens can also be included as part of the identification being used.

8. *Avoiding headphones*—Headphones tend to obstruct hearing and awareness of surroundings. While running and cycling, especially in areas where there may some traffic, it is best to avoid earphones. It may be a little dull in the initial stages but gradually one starts to enjoy the diversity and freshness that accompanies sounds of nature.

9. *Awareness of flora and fauna*—The experience of running and hiking in wooded and forested areas is quite refreshing. However, there is an element of risk associated with such experiences. While it may not be possible to completely eliminate all risks, it is advisable to at least be aware of any dangers and avoid them as far as possible. For example, on a trail run, it is recommended that marked trails that are commonly used be made use of rather than exploring uncharted territories when alone.

10. *Others*—Numerous other precautions in relation to physical fitness and nutrition have been discussed in previous sections. Staying hydrated at all times and ensuring a proper warm-up are examples of simple steps which, if not taken care of, can be quite dangerous. There are numerous other specific precautions that should be taken for each sport. Experts should be consulted in case any clarifications are required and appropriate preparation should be done.

SUMMARY

Fitness through an active lifestyle and outdoor pursuit activities has many benefits as explained in this workbook. The role of the fitness professional is to integrate technological tools and outdoor pursuit activities into the client's fitness programs. Your client can see you at the fitness facility two or three times a week and the rest of the time your clients can be doing outdoor pursuit activities following these progressions to achieve their fitness goals. As fitness professional using outdoor activities, it is important to think about sequencing the "workouts" the same way we sequence exercises when we design fitness programs. Starting with low intensity activities and having your client take a class with a professional in the outdoor pursuit industry are two ways to would lead to fitness program adherences.

Please share your success stories with me at josehgonzalez@live.com

HANDOUTS

DAILY LIFESTYLE LOG

Day - _____ Date -_____

	Perceived Difficulty	Plan Adherence	Performance Quality	Overall Satisfaction Score
Physical Activity	7	10	8	8
Workout Session	5	10	9	9
Diet & Nutrition	3	6	4	4
Sleep				
Mental Exercises				
Stress Management				
Attitude				

All parameters need to be rated on a scale of 1–10, 1 being lowest and 10 being highest.

WORKOUT SESSION LOG

Sr. No.	Name of Exercise	Number of Sets	Number of Repetitions	Tempo	Performance Tracker
1.	Joint Rotations set	1	5	-	Done
2.	Warm–up set				
	(A) Push–ups	1	6 – 10	111	Done
	(B) Squats	1	12 – 15	111	Done
	(C) Walk/ Run	1	10 minutes	Slow (3.0 – 4.0 mph)	Done
3.	Running	1	75 – 90 minutes	Moderate (6.5 to 7.0 mph)	75 minutes @ 7.2 mph average
4.	Cool–down set				Done
	(A) Walk/ Run	1	5 minutes	Slow (2.5 – 3.5 mph)	Done
5.	Static Stretching set	1	1	20 second hold	Done

* In all the cells, actual performance needs to be marked with a red pen.

DIET JOURNAL ENTRY

Meal Name	Time of Meal	Food Item	Quantity	Degree of Hunger
Breakfast	7:00 AM	Chicken Sandwich	1 no.	Low
		Tofu	60 grams	
		Fresh fruit salad	1 cup	
		Milk	300 ml.	
Pre – workout	10:00 AM	Oats	45 grams	Moderate
		Milk	200 ml.	
		Apple	1 no.	
Rating – (Rate adherence to diet plan on a scale of 1 to 10, 1 being the lowest)				
Comments – Subjective information in relation to diet adherence				

OUTDOOR PURSUIT ACTIVITIES
FOR FITNESS LOG

	Mon.	Tues.	Wed.	Thurs.	Friday	Sat.	Sun.
Week 1	Bike to work	Outdoor run and strength training	Bike to work	Outdoor run and strength training	Bike to work	Rest	Hike
Week 2	Bike to work	Outdoor run and strength training	Bike to work	Outdoor run and strength training	Bike to work	Paddle	Rest
Week 3	Bike to work	Outdoor run and strength training	Bike to work	Outdoor run and strength training	Bike to work	Rest	Hike
Week 4	Bike to work	Outdoor run and strength training	Bike to work	Outdoor run and strength training	Bike to work	Paddle	Rest
Week 5	Bike to work	Outdoor run and strength training	Bike to work	Outdoor run and strength training	Bike to work	Rest	Hike

REFERENCES

1. ACSM's Resource for the Personal Trainer – Second Edition, American College of Sports Medicine, www.acsm.org

2. ACE Personal Trainer Manual: The Ultimate Resource for Fitness Professionals, American Council on Exercise, www.acefitness.org

3. Rip Empson, The Ultimate Guide To The 50+ Hottest Health And Fitness Apps, Gadgets And Startups Of The Year, January 2nd, 2013, http://techcrunch.com/2013/01/02/best-health-apps/

4. Jill Duffy, Get Organized: Fitness Resolutions Through Technology, December 31st, 2012, http://www.pcmag.com/article2/0,2817,2413653,00.asp

5. Dr.Mercola, Can Technology Help You To Lose Weight?, January 25, 2013, http://fitness.mercola.com/sites/fitness/archive/2013/01/25/technology-gadgets.aspx

6. Wikipedia, Cardiovascular Fitness, http://en.wikipedia.org/wiki/Cardiovascular_fitness

7. Amanda Hynes, July 31st, 2011, 5 Activities to Improve Muscular Strength, http://www.livestrong.com/article/506101-5-activities-to-improve-muscular-strength/

8. Wikipedia, Flexibility, http://en.wikipedia.org/wiki/Flexibility_%28anatomy%29

9. Michael Esco, Stretching and Flexibility: 7 Tips, http://www.webmd.com/fitness-exercise/features/ stretching-and-flexibility-tips

10. Patrcik Dale, Definition of Muscular Strength and Endurance, March 28th, 2012, http://www.livestrong.com/ article/106346-definition-muscular-strength-endurance/

11. Jeffrey Janot, Comparing Intensity-Monitoring Methods, April 2005, http://www.ideafit.com/fitness-library/ comparing-intensity-monitoring-methods-0

12. John Kelly, How Leg Workouts for Runners Work, http://adventure.howstuffworks.com/outdoor-activities/running/training/leg-workouts-for-runners.htm

13. Dane Fletcher, Muscle-Building Outdoor Activities, July 12th, 2007, http://www.articlecity.com/articles/recreation_and_sports/ article_2918.shtml

14. Martin Bradstreet, Health Benefits Of Rock Climbing, 17 April, 2012, http://healthitude.net/health-benefits-of-rock-climbing. html

15. Wikipedia, Rock Climbing, http://en.wikipedia.org/wiki/ Rock_climbing

16. Lisa Larsen, How Many Muscles Do You Use When Surfing?, April 12th, 2010, http://www.mademan.com/mm/how-many-muscles-do-you-use-when-surfing.html#vply=0

17. Jones AM, Doust JH., Chelsea School Research Centre, University of Brighton, Eastbourne, UK., A 1% treadmill grade most

accurately reflects the energetic cost of outdoor running., August, 1996, http://www.ncbi.nlm.nih.gov/pubmed/8887211

18. Gretchen Reynolds, The Benefits of Exercising Outdoors, February 21st, 2013, http://well.blogs.nytimes.com/2013/02/21/the-be...

19. Logan AC, Selhub EM., Vis Medicatrix naturae: does nature "minister to the mind"?, April 3rd, 2012, http://www.ncbi.nlm.nih.gov/pubmed/22472137

ABOUT THE AUTHOR

Jose Gonzalez, Ed.D. —Jose has been involved in outdoor pursuit activities for more than 20 years. He grew up in Puerto Rico surfing, climbing and mountain biking. He worked for Outward Bound for 12 years, teaching sea kayaking and sailing expeditions. Jose has taught at various colleges in the USA, courses related to Active Lifestyles for 10 years. At Plymouth State University, Jose managed the fitness facility and staff as part of his Director of Campus Recreation duties. Jose considers himself a recreational athlete and has run the Lake Geneva marathon and has completed multiple Stand up Paddleboarding races, including the Battle of the Paddle in Dana Point California. Jose is an ACE Certified Personal Trainer and most recently he was filmed by REI for the Nature's Gym video series.

Printed in Great Britain
by Amazon

11203573R00086